TO BURN

WITH THE SPIRIT

OF CHRIST

Daily Readings on the Role of the Laity
in the Church

From the Documents of Vatican II

Rev. Nicholas Schneider

LIGUORI PUBLICATIONS
Liguori, Missouri 63057

Imprimi Potest:
Daniel L. Lowery, C.SS.R.
Provincial, St. Louis Province
Redemptorist Fathers
October 1, 1971

Imprimatur:
St. Louis, October 4, 1971
+ George J. Gottwald
Vicar General of St. Louis

Library of Congress Catalog Card Number: 70-183355

To my mother
who throughout her life
has burned with the spirit of Christ

Key to Sources

TABLE OF CONTENTS

The title — TO BURN WITH THE SPIRIT OF CHRIST — is found in the "Decree on the Apostolate of the Laity," N. 2.

Introduction

The lay apostolate has existed in the Church from the time of Christ, but Vatican II was the first council to deal with it explicitly. The thrust of this Council was to the Church's pastoral work among men. Since laymen are the authentic presence of the Church in the modern world, it was essential at this point of history that their role be clearly defined.

The Decree on the Apostolate of the Laity addressed itself specifically to the responsibilities of laymen, but many of the other documents also include statements regarding the duties of lay people as members of the Body of Christ. However, it is somewhat difficult to locate them in the mass of materials in which they are imbedded.

This book presents the pertinent statements of Vatican II concerning lay people, divided into 12 chapters and arranged as short readings, one for each day of the year. Each chapter is prefaced with a synopsis of its contents together with a schema of its development, and questions for discussion have been placed at the end of each chapter. A solid and broad theology of the laity is contained in this collection and its study will reveal the splendor of the lay apostolate in the Church.

I wish to thank the Redemptorist Fathers Christopher Farrell and Joseph Powers for their helpful suggestions for its improvements, and the editors of the America Press for permission to use their translation of the documents of the Second Vatican Council.

Father Nicholas Schneider
Easter 1971

JANUARY: PEOPLE OF GOD

SYNOPSIS

Vatican II canonized the term "People of God" as a description of the Church. This title embraces all its members, clerics, religious, and lay people. These latter are "fellow workers for the truth," and as sharers in the priesthood, prophetic mission and kingliness of Christ, they have an active role to play in the work of the Church.

Called as they are to permeate the world, and fortified by parish community life centered on the Eucharist, laymen must expend their energy for the Church's growth and sanctification.

All members of the Church bear equally the task of building up the Body of Christ. Pastors are to dialogue with their people and encourage them to use their talents for initiating projects which laymen judge to be needed. While laymen must obey their pastors, these leaders, in turn, must recognize the true·liberty enjoyed by all the children of God.

The Holy Spirit pours into the faithful His gifts and charisms for the good of mankind.

DEVELOPMENT

A new People (1 through 8).

Patterned on the dying Christ (9 through 11).

The priesthood of the faithful (12 and 13).

Diversity in the Church (14 and 15).

The parish community (16 through 18).

Dialogue between pastors and people (19 through 24).

Laymen constantly at work (25 and 26).

Apostles led by the Spirit (27 through 31).

JANUARY
PEOPLE OF GOD

A New People

1.

Christ the Lord, High Priest taken from among men (cf. Heb. 5:1-5), "made a kingdom and priests to God his Father" (Rev. 1:6; cf. 5:9-10) out of this new people. The baptized, by regeneration and the anointing of the Holy Spirit, are consecrated into a spiritual house and a holy priesthood. Thus through all those works befitting Christian men they can offer spiritual sacrifices and proclaim the power of Him who has called them out of darkness into His marvelous light (cf. 1 Pet. 2:4-10). Therefore all the disciples of Christ, persevering in prayer and praising God (cf. Acts 2:42-47), should present themselves as living sacrifice, holy and pleasing to God (cf. Rom. 12:1). Everywhere on earth they must bear witness to Christ and give an answer to those who seek an account of that hope of eternal life which is in them (cf. 1 Pet. 3:15) (DCC, N. 10).

2.

The mission of the Church concerns the salvation of men, which is to be achieved by belief in Christ and by His grace. Hence the apostolate of the Church and of all her members is primarily designed to manifest Christ's message by words and deeds and to communicate His grace to the world. This work is done mainly through the ministry of the Word and of the sacraments, which are entrusted in a special way to the clergy. But the laity too have their very important roles to play if they are to be "fellow workers for the truth" (3 John 8). It is especially on this level that the apostolate of the laity and the pastoral ministry complement one another (DAL, N. 6).

3.
The holy People of God shares also in Christ's prophetic office. It spreads abroad a living witness to Him, especially by means of a life of faith and charity and by offering to God a sacrifice of praise, the tribute of lips which give honor to His name (cf. Heb. 13:15). The body of the faithful as a whole, anointed as they are by the holy One (cf. John 2:20, 27), cannot err in matters of belief. Thanks to a supernatural sense of the faith which characterizes the People as a whole, it manifests this unerring quality when, "from the bishops down to the last member of the laity," (St. Augustine) it shows universal agreement in matters of faith and morals. For, by this sense of faith which is aroused and sustained by the Spirit of truth, God's People accept not the word of men, but the very Word of God (cf. 1 Th. 2:13). It clings without fail to the faith once delivered to the saints (cf. Jude 3), penetrates it more deeply by accurate insights, and applies it more thoroughly to life. All this it does under the lead of a sacred teaching authority to which it loyally defers (DCC, N. 12).

4.
As sharers in the role of Christ the priest, the prophet, and the king, the laity have an active part to play in the life and activity of the Church. Their activity is so necessary within the Church communities that without it the apostolate of the pastors is generally unable to achieve its full effectiveness. In the style of the men and women who helped Paul to spread the Gospel (cf. Acts 18:18, 26; Rom. 16:3), the laity with the right apostolic

attitude supply what is lacking in their brethren (cf. 1 Cor. 16:17, 18). Strengthened by active participation in the liturgical life of their community, they are eager to do their share in the apostolic works of that community. They lead to the Church people who are perhaps far removed from it, earnestly cooperate in presenting the Word of God especially by means of catechetical instruction, and offer their special skills to make the care of souls and the administration of the temporalities of the Church more efficient (DAL, N. 10).

5.
All men are called to belong to the new People of God. Wherefore this People, while remaining one and unique, is to be spread throughout the whole world and must exist in all ages, so that the purpose of God's will may be fulfilled. In the beginning God made human nature one. After His children were scattered, He decreed that they should at length be unified again (cf. John 11:52). It was for this reason that God sent His Son, whom He appointed heir of all things (cf. Heb. 1:2), that He might be teacher, king, and priest of all, the head of the new and universal people of the sons of God. For this God finally sent His Son's Spirit as Lord and lifegiver. He it is who, on behalf of the whole Church and each and every one of those who believe, is the principle of their coming together and remaining together in the teaching of the apostles and in fellowship, in the breaking of bread and in prayer (cf. Acts 2:42, Greek text) (DCC, N. 13).

6.
Therefore, the chosen People of God is one: "One Lord, one faith, one baptism" (Eph. 4:5). As members, they share a common dignity from their

rebirth in Christ. They have the same filial grace and the same vocation to perfection. They possess in common one salvation, one hope, and one undivided charity. Hence, there is in Christ and in the Church no inequality on the basis of race or nationality, social condition or sex, because "there is neither Jew nor Greek; there is neither slave nor freeman; there is neither male nor female. For you are all 'one' in Christ Jesus" (Gal. 3:28, Greek text; cf. Col. 3:11) (DCC, N. 32).

7.
It follows that among all the nations of earth there is but one People of God, which takes its citizens from every race, making them citizens of a kingdom which is of a heavenly and not an earthly nature. For all the faithful scattered throughout the world are in communion with each other in the Holy Spirit, so that "he who occupies the See of Rome knows the people of India are his members" (St. John Chrysostom). Since the kingdom of Christ is not of this world (cf. John 18:36), the Church or People of God takes nothing away from the temporal welfare of any people by establishing that kingdom. Rather does she foster and take to herself, insofar as they are good, the ability, resources, and customs of each people. Taking them to herself she purifies, strengthens, and ennobles them (DCC, N. 13).

8.
While she transcends all limits of time and race, the Church is destined to extend to all regions of the earth and so to enter the history of mankind. Moving forward through trial and tribulation, the Church is strengthened by the power of God's grace promised to her by the Lord, so that in the weakness of the flesh she may not waver from

perfect fidelity, but remain a bride worthy of her Lord; that moved by the Holy Spirit she may never cease to renew herself, until through the cross she arrives at the light which knows no setting (DCC, N. 9).

Patterned on the Dying Christ

9.

Since Jesus, the Son of God, manifested His charity by laying down His life for us, no one has greater love than he who lays down his life for Christ and his brothers (cf. 1 John 3:16; John 15:13). From the earliest times, then, some Christians have been called upon — and some will always be called upon — to give this supreme testimony of love to all men, but especially to persecutors. The Church, therefore, considers martyrdom as an exceptional gift and as the highest proof of love.

By martyrdom a disciple is transformed into an image of his Master, who freely accepted death on behalf of the world's salvation; he perfects that image even to the shedding of blood. Though few are presented with such an opportunity, nevertheless all must be prepared to confess Christ before men, and to follow Him along the way of the cross through the persecutions which the Church will never fail to suffer (DCC, N. 42).

10.

Pressing upon the Christian, to be sure, are the need and the duty to battle against evil through manifold tribulations and even to suffer death. But, linked with the paschal mystery and patterned on the dying Christ, he will hasten forward to resurrection in the strength which comes from hope (CCMW, N. 22).

11.

The laity are gathered together in the People of God and make up the Body of Christ under one head. Whoever they are, they are called upon, as living members, to expend all their energy for the growth of the Church and its continuous sanctification. For this very energy is a gift of the creator and a blessing of the redeemer (DCC, N. 33).

The Priesthood of the Faithful

12.

Though they differ from one another in essence and not only in degree, the common priesthood of the faithful and the ministerial or hierarchical priesthood are nonetheless interrelated. Each of them in its own special way is a participation in the one priesthood of Christ. The ministerial priest, by the sacred power he enjoys, molds and rules the priestly people. Acting in the person of Christ, he brings about the Eucharistic sacrifice, and offers it to God in the name of all the people. For their part, the faithful join in the offering of the Eucharist by virtue of their royal priesthood. They likewise exercise that priesthood by receiving the sacraments, by prayer and thanksgiving, by the witness of a holy life, and by self-denial and active charity (DCC, N. 10).

13.

It is through the sacraments and the exercise of the virtues that the sacred nature and organic structure of the priestly community is brought into operation. Incorporated into the Church through Baptism, the faithful are consecrated by the baptismal character to the exercise of the cult of the Christian religion. Reborn as sons of God, they must confess before men the faith which they have received from God through the Church.

Bound more intimately to the Church by the sacrament of Confirmation, they are endowed by the Holy Spirit with special strength. Hence they are more strictly obliged to spread and defend the faith both by word and by deed as true witnesses of Christ (DCC, N. 11).

Diversity in the Church

14.

By divine institution Holy Church is structured and governed with a wonderful diversity. "For just as in one body we have many members, yet all the members have not the same function, so we, the many, are one body in Christ, but severally members one of another" (Rom. 12:4, 5) (DCC, N. 32).

15.

While preserving unity in essentials, let all members of the Church, according to the office entrusted to each, preserve a proper freedom in the various forms of spiritual life and discipline, in the variety of liturgical rites, and even in the theological elaborations of revealed truth. In all things let charity be exercised. If the faithful are true to this course of action, they will be giving ever richer expression to the authentic catholicity of the Church, and, at the same time, to her apostolicity (DE, N. 4).

The Parish Community

16.

Offering an obvious example of the apostolate on the community level is the parish, inasmuch as it brings together the many human differences found within its boundaries and draws them into the universality of the Church. The laity should accustom themselves to working in the parish in close union with their priests, bringing to the Church community their own and the world's problems as well as questions concerning human salvation, all of which should be examined and resolved by common deliberation. As far as possible, the laity ought to collaborate energetically in every apostolic and missionary undertaking sponsored by their local parish (DPF, N. 10).

17.
No Christian community, however, can be built up unless it has its basis and center in the celebration of the most holy Eucharist. Here, therefore, all education in the spirit of community must originate. If this celebration is to be sincere and thorough, it must lead to various works of charity and mutual help, as well as to missionary activity and to different forms of Christian witness (DPF, N. 6).

18.
Moreover, by charity, prayer, example, and works of penance, the Church community exercises a true motherhood toward souls who are to be led to Christ. For this community constitutes an effective instrument by which the path to Christ and His Church is pointed out and made smooth for unbelievers, and by which the faithful are aroused, nourished, and strengthened for spiritual combat (DPF, N. 6).

Dialogue Between Pastors and People
19.
The laity have the right, as do all Christians, to receive in abundance from their sacred pastors the spiritual goods of the Church, especially the assis-

tance of the Word of God and the sacraments. Every layman should openly reveal to them his needs and desires with that freedom and confidence which befits a son of God and a brother in Christ. An individual layman, by reason of the knowledge, competence, or outstanding ability which he may enjoy, is permitted and sometimes even obliged to express his opinion on things which concern the good of the Church. When occasions arise, let this be done through the agencies set up by the Church for this purpose. Let it always be done in truth, in courage and in prudence, with reverence and charity toward those who by reason of their sacred office represent the person of Christ (DCC, N. 37).

20.

Let sacred pastors recognize and promote the dignity as well as the responsibility of the layman in the Church. Let them willingly make use of his prudent advice. Let them confidently assign duties to him in the service of the Church, allowing him freedom and room for action. Further, let them encourage the layman so that he may undertake tasks on his own initiative. Attentively in Christ, let them consider with fatherly love the projects, suggestions, and desires proposed by the laity. Furthermore, let pastors respectfully acknowledge that just freedom which belongs to everyone in this earthly city (DCC, N. 37).

21.

For the distinction which the Lord made between sacred ministers and the rest of the People of God entails a unifying purpose, since pastors and the other faithful are bound to each other by a mutual need. Pastors of the Church, following the example of the Lord, should minister to one another and to the faithful. The faithful in their turn should enthusiastically lend their cooperative assistance to their pastors and teachers. Thus in their diversity all bear witness to the admirable unity of the Body of Christ. This very diversity of graces, ministries, and works gathers the children of God into one, because "all these things are the work of one and the same Spirit" (1 Cor. 12:11) (DCC, N. 32).

22.

If therefore everyone in the Church does not proceed by the same path, nevertheless all are called to sanctity and have received an equal privilege of faith through the justice of God (cf. 2 Peter 1:1). And if by the will of God some are made teachers, dispensers of mysteries, and shepherds on behalf of others, yet all share a true equality with regard to the dignity and to the activity common to all the faithful for the building up of the Body of Christ (DCC, N. 32).

23.

With ready Christian obedience, laymen as well as all disciples of Christ should accept whatever their sacred pastors, as representatives of Christ, decree in their role as teachers and rulers in the Church. Let laymen follow the example of Christ, who, by His obedience even at the cost of death, opened to all men the blessed way to the liberty of the children of God. Nor should they omit to pray to God for those placed over them, who keep watch as having to render an account for their souls, so that they may render this account with joy and not with grief (cf. Heb. 13:17) (DCC, N. 37).

24.

A great many benefits are to be hoped for from this familiar dialogue between the laity and their pastors: in the laity, a strengthened sense of personal responsibility, a renewed enthusiasm, a more ready application of their talents to the projects of their pastors. The latter, for their part, aided by the experience of the laity, can more clearly and more suitably come to decisions regarding spiritual and temporal matters. In this way, the whole Church, strengthened by each one of its members, can more effectively fulfill its mission for the life of the world (DCC, N. 37).

Laymen Constantly at Work

25.

Since we know not the day nor the hour, on our Lord's advice we must constantly stand guard. Thus when we have finished the one and only course of our earthly life (cf. Heb. 9:27) we may merit to enter into the marriage feast with Him and to be numbered among the blessed (cf. Matt. 25:31-46). Thus we may not be commanded to go into eternal fire (cf. Matt. 25:41) like the wicked and slothful servant (cf. Matt. 25:26), into the exterior darkness where "there will be the weeping and the gnashing of teeth" (Matt. 22:13; 25:30). For before we reign with the glorious Christ, all of us will be made manifest "before the tribunal of Christ, so that each one will receive what he has won through the body, according to his works, whether good or evil" (2 Cor. 5:10). At the end of the world, "they who have done good shall come forth unto resurrection of life; but who have done evil unto resurrection of judgment" (John 5:29; cf. Matt. 25:46) (DCC, N. 48).

26.

We reckon therefore that "the sufferings of the present time are not worthy to be compared with

the glory to come that will be revealed in us"
(Rom. 8:18; cf. 2 Tim. 2:11-12). Strong in faith
we look for "the blessed hope and glorious coming
of our great God and Savior, Jesus Christ" (Tit.
2:13) "who will refashion the body of our lowli-
ness, conforming it to the body of his glory" (Phil.
3:21) and who will come "to be glorified in his
saints, and to be marveled at in all those who have
believed" (2 Thess. 1:10) (DCC, N. 48).

Apostles Led By the Spirit

27.
The Christian man, conformed to the likeness of
that Son who is the first-born of many brothers,
receives "the first-fruits of the Spirit" (Rom. 8:23)
by which he becomes capable of discharging the
new law of love. Through this Spirit, who is "the
pledge of our inheritance" (Eph. 1:14), the whole
man is renewed from within, even to the achievement of "the redemption of the body" (Rom.
8:23): "If the Spirit of him who raised Jesus from
the dead dwells in you, then he who raised Jesus
Christ from the dead will also bring to life your
mortal bodies because of his Spirit who dwells in
you" (Rom. 8:11) (CCMW, N. 22).

28.
Joined with Christ in the Church and signed with
the Holy Spirit "who is the pledge of our inheritance" (Eph. 1:14), we are truly called sons of God
and such we are (cf. 1 John 3:1). But we have not
yet appeared with Christ in the state of glory (cf.
Col. 3:4), in which we shall be like to God, since
we shall see Him as He is (cf. 1 John 3:2). Therefore, "while we are in the body, we are exiled
from the Lord" (2 Cor. 5:6), and having the first

fruits of the Spirit we groan within ourselves (cf. Rom. 8:23) and desire to be with Christ (cf. Phil. 1:23). A common love urges us to live more for Him, who died for us and rose again (cf. 2 Cor. 5:15). We strive therefore to please the Lord in all things (cf. 2 Cor. 5:9). We put on the armor of God that we may be able to stand against the wiles of the devil and resist on the evil day (cf. Eph. 6:11-13) (DCC, N. 48).

29.

The People of God believes that it is led by the Spirit of the Lord, who fills the earth. Motivated by this faith, it labors to decipher authentic signs of God's presence and purpose in the happenings, needs, and desires in which this People has a part along with other men of our age. For faith throws a new light on everything, manifests God's design for man's total vocation, and thus directs the mind to solutions which are fully human (CCMW, N. 11).

30.

For the exercise of this apostolate, the Holy Spirit who sanctifies the People of God through the ministry and the sacraments gives to the faithful special gifts as well (cf. 1 Cor. 12:7), "allotting to everyone according as he will" (1 Cor. 12:11). Thus may the individual, "according to the gift that each has received, administer it to one another" and become "good stewards of the manifold grace of God" (1 Peter 4:10), and build up thereby the whole body in charity (cf. Eph. 4:16). From the reception of these charisms or gifts, including those which are less dramatic, there arise for each believer the right and duty to use them in the Church and in the world for the good of mankind and for the upbuilding of the Church. In so doing, believers need to enjoy the freedom of the Holy Spirit who "breathes where he wills" (John 3:8). At the same time, they must act in communion with their brothers in Christ, especially with their pastors. The latter must make a judgment about the true nature and proper use of these gifts, not in order to extinguish the Spirit, but to test all things and hold fast to what is good (cf. 1 Thess. 5:12, 19, 21) (DAL, N. 3).

31.
As all the members of the human body, though they are many, form one body, so also are the faithful in Christ (cf. 1 Cor. 12:12). Also, in the building up of Christ's Body, there is a flourishing variety of members and functions. There is only one Spirit who, according to His own richness and the needs of the ministries, distributes His different gifts for the welfare of the Church (cf. 1 Cor. 12:1-11). Among these gifts stands out the grace given to the apostles. To their authority, the Spirit himself subjected even those who were endowed with charisms (cf. 1 Cor. 14). Giving the Body unity through himself and through His power and through the internal cohesion of its members, this same Spirit produces and urges love among the believers. Consequently, if one member suffers anything, all the members suffer too, and if one member is honored, all the members rejoice together (cf. 1 Cor. 12:26) (DCC, N. 7).

POINTS TO PONDER

To what are laymen consecrated by Baptism? (1 and 2)

How necessary is their role in the Church? (3 and 4)

Who are called by God to form His People? (5 through 8)

What does God expect of His People? (9 through 18)

How necessary is dialogue between laymen and their pastors? (19 through 25)

How seriously should laymen take their Christian obligations? (26 and 27)

How does the Holy Spirit assist the members of the Church? (28 through 31)

FEBRUARY: CALL TO HOLINESS

SYNOPSIS

"You are therefore to be perfect, even as your heavenly Father is perfect." The Lord addressed these words to all of His disciples. He gave them the example; He pours into them His love. The Holy Spirit dwells in the hearts of the faithful to enable them to accomplish their mission. Through Him all of the activities of life can become spiritual sacrifices.

All laymen are called to the fullness of Christian life and perfection of charity, lived out from day to day as they struggle to mold themselves into the image of Christ. True holiness consists in their devoting themselves with all of their being to the glory of God and the service of their neighbor.

By the power of the paschal mystery, the faithful are strengthened to show forth the Lord's love to the world. The sacraments, particularly the Eucharist, provide vitality for this task. Prayer, self-denial, active brotherly service and the exercise of the virtues complete the program of Christian holiness.

In Mary, laymen find the perfect model of the life to which they are called.

DEVELOPMENT

Christ has called His People to holiness (1 through 4).

The Holy Spirit supplies this holiness (5 through 7).

All are invited to pursue holiness (8 through 13).

Christ as the source of holiness (14 through 17).

Christian response to this holiness (18 through 21).

The sacraments and holiness (22 through 25).

Other means of holiness (26 through 28).

Mary as an inspiration to holiness (29).

FEBRUARY
CALL TO HOLINESS

Christ's Call to Holiness

1.

The Lord Jesus, the divine teacher and model of all perfection, preached holiness of life to each and every one of His disciples, regardless of their situation. "You therefore are to be perfect, even as your heavenly Father is perfect" (Matt. 5:48). He himself stands as the author and finisher of this holiness of life. For He sent the Holy Spirit upon all men that He might inspire them from within to love God with their whole heart and their whole soul, with all their mind and all their strength (cf. Mark 12:30) and that they might love one another as Christ loved them (cf. John 13:34; 15:12) (DCC, N. 40).

2.

Undergoing death itself for all of us sinners, He taught us by example that we too must shoulder that cross which the world and the flesh inflict upon those who search after peace and justice. Appointed Lord by His Resurrection and given plenary power in heaven and on earth, Christ is now at work in the hearts of men through the energy of His Spirit. He arouses not only a desire for the age to come, but, by that very fact, He animates, purifies, and strengthens those noble longings too by which the human family strives to make its life more human and to render the whole earth submissive to this goal (CCMW, N. 38).

3.

The Son, therefore, came on mission from His Father. It was in Him, before the foundation of the world, that the Father chose us and pre-destined us to become adopted sons, for in Him it has pleased the Father to reestablish all things (cf. Eph. 1:4, 5, 10). To carry out the will of the Father, Christ inaugurated the kingdom of heaven on earth and revealed to us the mystery of the Father. By His obedience He brought about re-demption. The Church, or in other words, the kingdom of Christ now present in mystery, grows visibly in the world through the power of God (DCC, N. 3).

4.

"God is love, and he who abides in love abides in God, and God in him" (1 John 4:16). God pours out His love into our hearts through the Holy Spirit, who has been given to us (cf. Rom. 5:5). Thus the first and most necessary gift is that charity by which we love God above all things and our neighbor because of God. If that love, as good seed, is to grow and bring forth fruit in the soul, each one of the faithful must willingly hear the Word of God and with the help of His grace act to fulfill His will (DCC, N. 42).

The Holy Spirit Supplies Holiness

5.

The Spirit dwells in the Church and in the hearts of the faithful as in a temple (cf. 1 Cor. 3:16; 6:19). In them He prays and bears witness to the fact that they are adopted sons (cf. Gal. 4:6; Rom. 8:15, 16, 26). The Spirit guides the Church into the fullness of truth (cf. John 16:13) and gives her a unity of fellowship and service. He furnishes and directs her with various gifts, both hierarchical and charismatic, and adorns her with the fruits of His grace (cf. Eph. 4:11, 12; 1 Cor. 12:4; Gal. 5:22).

By the power of the Gospel He makes the Church grow, perpetually renews her, and leads her to perfect union with her spouse. The Spirit and the bride both say to the Lord Jesus, "Come!" (cf. Rev. 22:17) (DCC, N. 4).

6.
Now the gifts of the Spirit are diverse. He calls some to give clear witness to the desire for a heavenly home and to keep that desire green among the human family. He summons others to dedicate themselves to the earthly service of men and to make ready the material of the celestial realm by this ministry of theirs. Yet He frees all of them so that by putting aside love of self and bringing all earthly resources into the service of human life they can devote themselves to that future when humanity itself will become an offering accepted by God (CCMW, N. 38).

7.
Although by the power of the Holy Spirit, the Church has remained the faithful spouse of her Lord and has never ceased to be the sign of salvation on earth, still she is very aware that among her members, both clerical and lay, some have been unfaithful to the Spirit of God during the course of many centuries. In the present age, too, it does not escape the Church how great a distance lies between the message she offers and the human failings of those to whom the Gospel is entrusted (CCMW, N. 43).

All Invited to Holiness

8.
All of Christ's followers, therefore, are invited and bound to pursue holiness and the perfect fulfill-

ment of their proper state. Hence, let them all see that they guide their affections rightly. Otherwise, they will be thwarted in the search for perfect charity by the way they use earthly possessions and by a fondness for riches which goes against the Gospel spirit of poverty. The apostle has sounded a warning: Let those who make use of this world not get bogged down in it, for the structure of this world is passing away (cf. 1 Cor. 7:31, Greek text) (DCC, N. 42).

9.

Since the supreme and eternal priest, Jesus Christ, wills to continue His witness and serve through the laity, too, He vivifies them in His Spirit and unceasingly urges them on to every good and perfect work (DCC, N. 34).

10.

For besides intimately associating them with His life and His mission, Christ also gives them a share in His priestly function of offering spiritual worship for the glory of God and the salvation of men. For this reason the laity, dedicated to Christ and anointed by the Holy Spirit, are marvelously called and equipped to produce in themselves ever more abundant fruits of the Spirit. For all their works, prayers, and apostolic endeavors, their ordinary married and family life, their daily labor, their mental and physical relaxation, if carried out in the Spirit, and even the hardships of life, if patiently borne — all of these become spiritual sacrifices acceptable to God through Jesus Christ (cf. 1 Peter 2:5). During the celebration of the Eucharist, these sacrifices are most lovingly offered to the Father along with the Lord's body. Thus as worshipers whose every deed is holy, the laity consecrate the world itself to God (DCC, N. 34).

11.

This most sacred Council, then, earnestly entreats in the Lord that all laymen give a glad, generous, and prompt response to the voice of Christ, who is giving them an especially urgent invitation at this moment, and to the impulse of the Holy Spirit. Younger people should feel that this call has been directed to them in particular, and they should respond to it eagerly and magnanimously. Through this holy Synod, the Lord himself renews His invitation to all the laity to come closer to Him every day, and, recognizing that what is His is also their own (Phil. 2:5), to associate themselves with Him in His saving mission. Once again He sends them into every town and place where He himself will come (cf. Luke 10:1). Thus they can show that they are His co-workers in the various forms and methods of the Church's one apostolate, which must be constantly adapted to the new needs of the times. May they always abound in the works of God, knowing that they will not labor in vain when their labor is for Him (cf. 1 Cor. 15:58) (DAL, N. 33).

12.

The followers of Christ are called by God, not according to their accomplishments, but according to His own purpose and grace. They are justified in the Lord Jesus, and through Baptism sought in faith they truly become sons of God and sharers in the divine nature. In this way they are really made holy. Then, too, by God's gifts they must hold on to and complete in their lives this holiness which they have received. They are warned by the apostle to live "as becomes saints" (Eph. 5:3), and to put on "as God's chosen ones, holy and beloved, a heart of mercy, kindness, humility, meekness, patience" (Col. 3:12), and to possess the fruits of the Spirit unto holiness (cf. Gal. 5:22; Rom. 6:22). Since we all truly offend in many things (cf. Jas. 3:2), we all need God's mercy continuously and must daily pray: "Forgive us our debts" (Matt. 6:12) (DCC, N. 40).

13.

Thus it is evident to everyone that all the faithful of Christ of whatever rank or status are called to the fullness of the Christian life and to the perfection of charity. By this holiness a more human way of life is promoted even in this earthly society. In order that the faithful may reach this perfection, they must use their strength according as they have received it, as a gift from Christ. In this way they can follow in His footsteps and mold themselves in His image, seeking the will of the Father in all things, devoting themselves with all their being to the glory of God and the service of their neighbor. In this way too, the holiness of the People of God will grow into an abundant harvest of good, as is brilliantly proved by the lives of so many saints in Church history (DCC, N. 40).

Christ — Source of Holiness

14.

Having become the model of a man loving his wife as his own body, Christ loves the Church as His bride (cf. Eph. 5:25-28). For her part, the Church is subject to her head (cf. Eph. 5:22, 23). "For in him dwells all the fullness of the Godhead bodily" (Col. 2:9). He fills the Church, which is His Body and His fullness, with His divine gifts (cf. Eph.

1:22-23) so that she may grow and reach all the fullness of God (cf. Eph. 3:19) (DCC, N. 7).

15.
The head of this Body is Christ. He is the image of the invisible God and in Him all things came into being. He has priority over everyone and in Him all things hold together. He is the head of that Body which is the Church. He is the beginning, the firstborn from the dead, so that in all things He might have the first place (cf. Col. 1:15-18). By the greatness of His power He rules the things of heaven and the things of earth, and with His all-surpassing perfection and activity, He fills the whole Body with the riches of His glory (cf. Eph. 1:18-23) (DCC, N. 7).

16.
Now, this holiness of the Church is unceasingly manifested, as it ought to be, through those gifts of grace that the Spirit produces in the faithful. It is expressed in the multiple ways of life by those individuals who, in their walk of life, strive for the perfection of charity, and thereby help others to grow. In a particularly appropriate way this holiness shines out in the practice of the counsels customarily called "evangelical." Under the influence of the Holy Spirit, the practice of these counsels is undertaken by many Christians, either privately or in some Church-approved situation or state, and produces in the world, as it should, a shining witness and model of holiness (DCC, N. 39).

17.
From Him "the whole body, supplied and built up by joints and ligaments, attains a growth that is of

God" (Col. 2:19). He continually distributes in His Body, that is, the Church, gifts of ministries through which, by His own power, we serve each other unto salvation so that, carrying out the truth in love, we may through all things grow up into Him who is our head (cf. Eph. 4:11-16, Greek text) (DCC, N. 7).

Christian Response to Holiness

18.
The Church, "like a pilgrim in a foreign land, presses forward amid the persecutions of the world and the consolations of God," (St. Augustine) announcing the cross and death of the Lord until He comes (cf. 1 Cor. 11:26). By the power of the risen Lord, she is given strength to overcome patiently and lovingly the afflictions and hardships which assail her from within and without, and to show forth in the world the mystery of the Lord in a faithful though shadowed way, until at the last it will be revealed in total splendor (DCC, N. 8).

19.
Just as Christ carried out the work of redemption in poverty and under oppression, so the Church is called to follow the same path in communicating to men the fruits of salvation. Christ Jesus, "though he was by nature God . . . emptied himself, taking the nature of a slave" (Phil. 2:6), and "being rich, he became poor" (2 Cor. 8:9), for our sakes. Thus, although the Church needs human resources to carry out her mission, she is not set up to seek earthly glory, but to proclaim humility and self-sacrifice, even by her own example (DCC, N. 8).

20.

As members of the living Christ, all the faithful have been incorporated into Him and made like unto Him through Baptism, Confirmation, and the Eucharist. Hence all are duty bound to cooperate in the expansion and growth of His Body, so that they can bring it to fullness as swiftly as possible (Eph. 4:13) (DCMA, N. 36).

21.

All the members ought to be molded into Christ's image until He is formed in them (cf. Gal. 4:19). For this reason we who have been made like unto Him, who have died with Him and been raised up with Him, are taken up into the mysteries of His life, until we reign together with Him (cf. Phil. 3:21; 2 Tim. 2:11; Eph. 2:6; Col. 2:12; etc.). Still in pilgrimage upon the earth, we trace in trial and under oppression the paths He trod. Made one with His sufferings as the Body is one with the head, we endure with Him, that with Him we may be glorified (cf. Rom. 8:17) (DCC, N. 7).

Sacraments and Holiness

22.

This inauguration and this growth are both symbolized by the blood and water which flowed from the open side of the crucified Jesus (cf. John 19:34), and are foretold in the Lord's words concerning His death on the cross: "And I, if I be lifted up from the earth, will draw all men to myself" (John 12:32, Greek text). As often as the sacrifice of the cross in which "Christ, our passover, has been sacrificed" (1 Cor. 5:7) is celebrated on an altar, the work of our redemption is carried on. At the same time, in the sacrament of the Eucharistic bread the unity of all believers who form one body in Christ (cf. 1 Cor. 10:17) is both expressed and brought about. All men are called to this union with Christ, who is the light of the world, from whom we go forth, through whom we live, and toward whom our journey leads us (DCC, N. 3).

23.

Taking part in the Eucharistic sacrifice, which is the fount and apex of the whole Christian life, they (the faithful) offer the divine victim to God, and offer themselves along with it. Thus, both by the act of oblation and through holy Communion, all perform their proper part in this liturgical service, not, indeed, all in the same way, but each in that way which is appropriate to himself. Strengthened anew at the holy table by the Body of Christ, they manifest in a practical way that unity of God's People which is suitably signified and wondrously brought about by this most awesome sacrament (DCC, N. 11).

24.

The Church, therefore, earnestly desires that Christ's faithful, when present at this mystery of faith, should not be there as strangers or silent spectators. On the contrary, through a proper appreciation of the rites and prayers they should participate knowingly, devoutly, and actively. They should be instructed by God's Word and be refreshed at the table of the Lord's Body; they should give thanks to God; by offering the immaculate victim, not only through the hands of the priest, but also with him, they should learn to offer themselves too. Through Christ the mediator, they should be drawn day by day into ever closer

union with God and with each other, so that
finally God may be all in all (CSL, N. 48).

25.
Each must share frequently in the sacraments, the
Eucharist especially, and in liturgical rites. Each
must apply himself constantly to prayer, self-
denial, active brotherly service, and the exercise of
all the virtues. For charity, as the bond of perfection and the fulfillment of the law (cf. Col. 3:14;
Rom. 13:10), rules over all the means of attaining
holiness, gives life to them, and makes them work.
Hence it is the love of God and of neighbor which
points out the true disciple of Christ (DCC, N. 42).

Other Means of Holiness

26.
The spiritual life, however, is not confined to
participation in the liturgy. The Christian is assur-
edly called to pray with his brethren, but he must
also enter into his chamber and pray to the Father
in secret (cf. Matt. 6:6); indeed, according to the
teaching of the apostle Paul, he should pray without ceasing (cf. 1 Thess. 5:17). We learn from the
same apostle that we must always carry about in
our body the dying of Jesus, so that the life of
Jesus too may be made manifest in our bodily
frame (cf. 2 Cor. 4:10, 11). This is why we ask the
Lord in the sacrifice of the Mass that, "receiving
the offering of the spiritual victim," He may fashion us for himself "as an eternal gift" (Prayer over
the Gifts for Monday of Pentecost Week) (CSL, N.
12).

27.
It is not only through the sacraments and Church
ministries that the same Holy Spirit sanctifies and

leads the People of God and enriches it with virtues. Allotting His gifts "to everyone according as he will" (1 Cor. 12:11), He distributes special graces among the faithful of every rank. By these gifts He makes them fit and ready to undertake the various tasks or offices advantageous for the renewal and rebuilding of the Church, according to the words of the apostle: "The manifestation of the Spirit is given to everyone for profit" (1 Cor. 12:7). These charismatic gifts, whether they be the most outstanding or the more simple and widely diffused, are to be received with thanksgiving and consolation, for they are exceedingly suitable and useful for the needs of the Church (DCC, N. 12).

28.
Fortified by so many and such powerful means of salvation, all the faithful, whatever their condition or state, are called by the Lord, each in his own way, to that perfect holiness whereby the Father himself is perfect (DCC, N. 11).

Mary — Inspiration to Holiness

29.
In the most holy Virgin the Church has already reached that perfection whereby she exists without spot or wrinkle (cf. Eph. 5:27). Yet the followers of Christ still strive to increase in holiness by conquering sin. And so they raise their eyes to Mary who shines forth to the whole community of the elect as a model of the virtues. Devotedly meditating on her and contemplating her in the light of the Word made Man, the Church with reverence enters more intimately into the supreme mystery of the Incarnation and becomes ever increasingly like her spouse (DCC, N. 65).

POINTS TO PONDER

Who are called to holiness? (1 through 3)

What is the source of Christian life? (4 through 12)

How does Christ offer help to members of His Body? (13 through 22)

What importance has the Eucharist in the Christian vocation? (23 through 28)

How is Mary a model of perfection for us? (29)

MARCH: WITNESSES

SYNOPSIS

All laymen must stand before the world as witnesses to the Resurrection of the Lord and as signs that God lives in the midst of human society. This requires a living and mature faith founded upon an adequate understanding of the truth. To faith must be added hope and love, which compel Christians to make the divine message of salvation known to and accepted by all men.

The main duty of lay people, as new men created according to God in justice and true holiness, is to bear witness to Christ in their homes, their social groups, and their professional circles. To succeed, they must unite as closely as possible with the people of their time and country. They must also, as the occasion arises, announce Christ to unbelievers and to those who already believe in order to deepen their faith. In this way the spirit of the Gospel will penetrate all of life.

The witness of Christian lay life should touch all men, and certain key professions are especially useful for this. "Witness" is best described as a striving to generously and effectively serve the needs of men in the modern world.

DEVELOPMENT

Christ has called all of His members to be witnesses (1 through 5).

Each individual layman must give this witness (6 through 9).

Witness is best given by genuine Christian living (10 through 15).

At times the Gospel must be explicitly announced (16 through 19).

Some types of witness demand special formation (20 through 24).

All Christians should cooperate with one another in giving witness (25 through 29).

Witness means continual service (30 and 31).

MARCH
WITNESSES

Christ's Call to Witness

1.

Christ obeyed even at the cost of death, and was therefore raised up by the Father (cf. Phil. 2:8, 9). Thus He entered into the glory of His kingdom. To Him all things are made subject until He subjects himself and all created things to the Father, that God may be all in all (cf. 1 Cor. 15:27, 28). Now Christ has communicated this power of subjection to His disciples that they might be established in royal freedom and that by self-denial and a holy life they might conquer the reign of sin in themselves (cf. Rom. 6:12). Further, He has shared this power so that by serving Him in their fellow-men they might through humility and patience lead their brother men to that king whom to serve is to reign (DCC, N. 36).

2.

The greatest commandment in the law is to love God with one's whole heart and one's neighbor as oneself (cf. Matt. 22:37-40). Christ made this commandment of love of neighbor His own and enriched it with a new meaning. For He wanted to identify himself with His brethren as the object of this love when He said, "As long as you did it for one of these, the least of my brethren, you did it for me" (Matt. 25:40). Taking on human nature, He bound the whole human race to himself as a family through a certain supernatural solidarity and established charity as the mark of His disciples, saying, "By this will all men know that you are my disciples, if you have love for one another" (John 13:35) (DAL, N. 8).

3.

Whoever in obedience to Christ seeks first the kingdom of God will as a consequence receive a stronger and purer love for helping all his brothers and for perfecting the work of justice under the inspiration of charity (CCMW, N. 72).

4.

Since they have an active role to play in the whole life of the Church, laymen are not only bound to penetrate the world with a Christian spirit. They are also called to be witnesses to Christ in all things in the midst of human society (CCMW, N. 43).

5.

Impelled by divine charity, they do good to all men, especially to those of the household of the faith (cf. Gal. 6:10), laying aside "all malice and all deceit and pretense, and envy, and all slander" (1 Pet. 2:1), and thereby they draw men to Christ. This charity of God, which "is poured forth in our hearts by the Holy Spirit who has been given to us" (Rom. 5:5), enables the laity to express the true spirit of the beatitudes in their lives. Following Jesus who was poor, they are neither depressed by the lack of temporal goods, nor puffed up by their abundance. Imitating Christ who was humble, they have no obsession for empty honors (cf. Gal. 5:26), but seek to please God rather than men, ever ready to leave all things for Christ's sake (cf. Luke 14:26) and to suffer persecution for justice' sake (cf. Matt. 5:10). For they remember the words of the Lord, "If anyone wishes to come after me, let him deny himself, and take up his cross, and follow me" (Matt. 16:24). Promoting Christian friendship among themselves, they help one another in any kind of necessity (DAL, N. 4).

Each Must Give Witness

6.

Each individual layman must stand before the world as a witness to the Resurrection and life of the Lord Jesus and as a sign that God lives. As a body and individually, the laity must do their part to nourish the world with spiritual fruits (cf. Gal. 5:22), and to spread abroad in it that spirit by which are animated those poor, meek, and peace-making men whom the Lord in the Gospel calls blessed (cf. Matt. 5:3-9). In a word, "what the soul is to the body, let Christians be to the world" (St. John Chrysostom) (DCC, N. 38).

7.

This result is achieved chiefly by the witness of a living and mature faith, namely, one trained to see difficulties clearly and to master them. Very many martyrs have given luminous witness to this faith and continue to do so. This faith needs to prove its fruitfulness by penetrating the believer's entire life, including its worldly dimensions, and by activating him toward justice and love, especially regarding the needy. What does the most to reveal God's presence, however, is the brotherly love of the faithful who are united in spirit as they work together for the faith of the Gospel and who prove themselves as a sign of unity (CCMW, N. 21).

8.

The disciple is bound by a grave obligation toward Christ his master ever more adequately to understand the truth received from Him, faithfully to proclaim it, and vigorously to defend it, never — be it understood — having recourse to means that are incompatible with the spirit of the Gospel. At the same time, the charity of Christ urges him to act lovingly, prudently and patiently in his dealings with those who are in error or in ignorance with regard to the faith. All is to be taken into account — the Christian duty to Christ, the life-giving Word which must be proclaimed, the rights of the human person, and the measure of grace granted by God through Christ to men, who are invited freely to accept and profess the faith (DRF, N. 14).

9.

Thus, indeed, he may grow into manhood according to the mature measure of Christ (cf. Eph. 4:13), and devote himself to the upbuilding of the Mystical Body. Moreover, aware of his calling, he should grow accustomed to giving witness to the hope that is in him (1 Pet. 3:15), and to promoting that Christian transformation of the world by which natural values, viewed in the full perspective of humanity as redeemed by Christ, may contribute to the good of society as a whole (DCE, N. 2).

Witness by Christian Living

10.

The sacraments of the New Law, by which the life and apostolate of the faithful are nourished, prefigure a new heaven and a new earth (cf. Rev. 21:1). So too the laity go forth as powerful heralds of a faith in things to be hoped for (cf. Heb. 11:1), provided they steadfastly join their profession of faith to a life springing from faith. This evangelization, that is, this announcing of Christ by a living testimony as well as by the spoken word, takes on a specific quality and a special force in that it is carried out in the ordinary surroundings of the world (DCC, N. 35).

11.

The apostolate is carried out through the faith, hope, and charity which the Holy Spirit diffuses in the hearts of all members of the Church. Indeed, the law of love, which is the Lord's greatest commandment, impels all the faithful to promote God's glory through the spread of His kingdom and to obtain for all men that eternal life which consists in knowing the only true God and Him whom He sent, Jesus Christ (cf. John 17:3). On all Christians therefore is laid the splendid burden of working to make the divine message of salvation known and accepted by all men throughout the world (DAL, N. 3).

12.

Yet, let all realize that their first and most important obligation toward the spread of the faith is this: to lead a profoundly Christian life. For their fervor in the service of God and their charity toward others will cause a new spiritual inspiration to sweep over the whole Church. Then she will appear as a sign lifted up among the nations (cf. Is. 11:12), "the light of the world" (Matt. 5:14), and "the salt of the earth" (Matt. 5:13). This living testimony will more easily achieve its effect if it is given in unison with other Christian communities, according to the norms of the *Decree on Ecumenism* (DCMA, N. 36).

13.

Their main duty, whether they are men or women, is the witness which they are bound to bear to Christ by their life and works in the home, in their social group, and in their own professional circle. For in them there must appear the new man created according to God in justice and true holiness (cf. Eph. 4:24). But they must give expression to this newness of life in the social and cultural framework of their own homeland, according to their own national traditions. They must be acquainted with this culture. They must heal it and preserve it. They must develop it in accordance with modern conditions, and finally perfect it in Christ. Thus the faith of Christ and the life of the Church will no longer be something extraneous to the society in which they live, but it will begin to permeate and transform it (DCMA, N. 21).

14.
That they may be able to give this witness to Christ fruitfully, let them be joined to those men by esteem and love, and acknowledge themselves to be members of the group of men among whom they live. Let them share in cultural and social life by the various exchanges and enterprises of human living. Let them be familiar with their national and religious traditions, gladly and reverently laying bare the seeds of the Word which lie hidden in them (DCMA, N. 11).

15.
Upon all the laity, therefore, rests the noble duty of working to extend the divine plan of salvation ever increasingly to all men of each epoch and in every land. Consequently, let every opportunity be given to them so that, according to their abilities and the needs of the times, they may zealously participate in the saving work of the Church (DCC, N. 53).

Explicitly Announce Gospel
16.
However, an apostolate of this kind does not consist only in the witness of one's way of life; a true apostle looks for opportunities to announce Christ

by words addressed either to nonbelievers with a view to leading them to faith, or to believers with a view to instructing and strengthening them, and motivating them toward a more fervent life. "For the love of Christ impels us" (2 Cor. 5:14), and the words of the apostle should echo in every Christian heart: "For woe to me if I do not preach the gospel" (1 Cor. 9:16) (DAL, N. 6).

17.
There are innumerable opportunities open to the laity for the exercise of their apostolate of making the Gospel known and men holy. The very testimony of their Christian life, and good works done in a supernatural spirit, have the power to draw men to belief and to God; for the Lord says, "Even so let your light shine before men, in order that they may see your good works and give glory to your Father in heaven" (Matt. 5:16) (DAL, N. 6).

18.
They exercise a genuine apostolate by their activity on behalf of bringing the Gospel and holiness to men, and on behalf of penetrating the temporal sphere of things through the spirit of the Gospel. In this way, their temporal activity can openly bear witness to Christ and promote the salvation of men. Since it is proper to the layman's state in life for him to spend his days in the midst of the world and of secular transactions, he is called by God to burn with the spirit of Christ and to exercise his apostolate in the world as a kind of leaven (DAL, N. 2).

19.
This apostolate should reach out to all men wherever they can be found; it should not exclude any

spiritual or temporal benefit which can possibly be conferred. True apostles, however, are not content with this activity alone, but look for the opportunity to announce Christ through the spoken word as well. For there are many persons who can hear the Gospel and recognize Christ only through the laity who live near them (DAL, N. 13).

Witness Demands Special Formation

20.

Some types of the apostolate demand very special formation. When the apostolate is one of making the Gospel known and men holy, the laity must be specially formed to engage in conversation with others, believers or nonbelievers, in order to manifest Christ's message to all men. Since in our times, variations of materialism are rampant everywhere, even among Catholics, the laity should not only learn doctrine more carefully, especially those main points which are the subjects of controversy, but should also provide the witness of an evangelical life in contrast to all forms of materialism (DAL, N. 31).

21.

While every exercise of the apostolate should take its origin and power from charity, some works by their very nature can become especially vivid expressions of this charity. Christ the Lord wanted these works to be signs of His Messianic mission (cf. Matt. 11:4, 5) (DAL, N. 8).

22.

Christians who take an active part in modern socioeconomic development and defend justice and charity should be convinced that they can make a great contribution to the prosperity of mankind and the peace of the world. Whether they do so as individuals or in associations, let their example be a shining one. After acquiring whatever skills and experience are absolutely necessary, they should in faithfulness to Christ and His Gospel observe the right order of values in their earthly activities. Thus their whole lives, both individual and social, will be permeated with the spirit of the beatitudes, notably the spirit of poverty (CCMW, N. 72).

23.
Since, in this age of ours, new problems are arising and extremely serious errors are gaining currency which tend to undermine the foundations of religion, the moral order, and human society itself, this sacred Synod earnestly exhorts laymen, each according to his natural gifts and learning, to be more diligent in doing their part according to the mind of the Church, to explain and defend Christian principles, and to apply them rightly to the problems of our era (DAL, N. 6).

24.
At the same time, however, they should look to the profound changes which are taking place among nations. They should exert themselves lest modern man, overly intent on the science and technology of today's world, become a stranger to things divine. Rather, let them awaken in him a fiercer yearning for that truth and charity which God has revealed (DCMA, N. 11).

Cooperation Needed for Witness

25.
The common heritage of the Gospel and the common duty of Christian witness resulting from it recommend and frequently require the coopera-

tion of Catholics with other Christians, a cooperation exercised on the part of individuals and communities within the Church, either in activities or in associations, and on the national and international level (DAL, N. 27).

26.

The Church must be present in these groups of men through those of her children who dwell among them or are sent to them. For wherever they live, all Christians are bound to show forth, by the example of their lives and by the witness of their speech, that new man which they put on at Baptism, and that power of the Holy Spirit by whom they were strengthened at Confirmation. Thus other men, observing their good works, can glorify the Father (cf. Matt. 5:16) and can better perceive the real meaning of human life and the bond which ties the whole community of mankind together (DCMA, N. 11).

27.

Laymen cooperate in the Church's work of evangelization. As witnesses and at the same time as living instruments, they share in her saving mission. This is especially so if they have been called by God and have been accepted by the bishop for this work (DCMA, N. 41).

28.

Let all Christ's faithful remember that the more purely they strive to live according to the Gospel, the more they are fostering and even practicing Christian unity. For they can achieve depth and ease in strengthening mutual brotherhood to the degree that they enjoy profound communion with the Father, the Word, and the Spirit (DE, N. 7).

29.

Likewise, common human values not infrequently call for cooperation between Christians pursuing apostolic aims and men who do not profess Christ's name but acknowledge these values. By this dynamic and prudent cooperation, which is of special importance in temporal activities, the laity bear witness to Christ, the Savior of the world, as well as to the unity of the human family (DAL, N. 27).

Witness — Continual Service

30.

Mindful of the Lord's saying: "By this will all men know that you are my disciples, if you have love for one another" (John 13:35), Christians cannot yearn for anything more ardently than to serve the men of the modern world ever more generously and effectively. Therefore, holding faithfully to the Gospel and benefiting from its resources, and united with every man who loves and practices justice, Christians have shouldered a gigantic task demanding fulfillment in this world. Concerning this task, they must give a reckoning to Him who will judge every man on the last day (CCMW, N. 93).

31.

Not everyone who cries, "Lord, Lord," will enter into the kingdom of heaven, but those who do the Father's will and take a strong grip on the work at hand. Now, the Father wills that in all men we recognize Christ our brother and love Him effectively in word and in deed. By thus giving witness to the truth, we will share with others the mystery of the heavenly Father's love. As a consequence, men throughout the world will be aroused to a lively hope — the gift of the Holy Spirit — that they will finally be caught up in peace and utter happiness in that fatherland radiant with the splendor of the Lord (CCMW, N. 93).

POINTS TO PONDER

Why is love the hallmark of God's kingdom? (1 through 3)

Why must laymen bear witness to Christ in their lives? (4 through 6)

How is this work of witnessing carried out? (7 through 12)

What is the value of specifically lay witness? (13 through 19)

Why is special training often necessary? (20 through 24)

Should separated Christians witness together? (25 through 29)

What is the goal of all Christian witness? (30 and 31)

APRIL: INDIVIDUAL APOSTOLATE

SYNOPSIS

The success of the lay apostolate is directly dependent upon each layman's living union with Christ. All members of the Church are "laymen" except those in Holy Orders or in a religious group sanctioned by ecclesiastical authority. Their apostolate is a participation in the saving work of the Church. Incorporated into Christ through Baptism and strengthened through Confirmation, laymen are consecrated into a holy people and royal priesthood to offer spiritual sacrifices and to carry Christ into the world.

Every lay person is called to the individual apostolate inasmuch as it consists in living a life based upon faith, hope, and charity. This type of apostolate is needed particularly in areas of the world where religion is persecuted or suppressed.

The apostolic formation of laymen must correspond to their state of life and therefore it must have an acceptable element of secularity in it. Especially must they be trained to observe human conditions under which they live, judge them in the light of faith, and act to change them when necessary. In addition to spiritual formation, a thorough cultural education is required. From early childhood through the university, such formation must be available if true apostles are to be trained.

The hierarchy should promote the apostolate of the laity and allow it maximum freedom. Lay people, imitating the example of Mary, can exercise notable influence on their fellow-men by living in intimate union with Christ.

DEVELOPMENT

Every lay person is called to the apostolate (1 and 2).

Description of the lay apostolate (3 through 6).

How laymen engage in the individual apostolate (7 through 12).

Formation for the individual apostolate (13 through 19).

Education as a means of formation (20 through 22).

The hierarchy and the individual apostolate (23 through 27).

Christ as the focal point of the apostolate (28 and 29).

Mary as prototype for the individual apostolate (30).

INDIVIDUAL APOSTOLATE

All Called to Apostolate

1.

Since Christ in His mission from the Father is the fountain and source of the whole apostolate of the Church, the success of the lay apostolate depends upon the laity's living union with Christ. For the Lord has said, "He who abides in me, and I in him, he bears much fruit: for without me you can do nothing" (John 15:5). This life of intimate union with Christ in the Church is nourished by spiritual aids which are common to all the faithful, especially active participation in the sacred liturgy. These are to be used by the faithful in such a way that while properly fulfilling their secular duties in the ordinary conditions of life, they do not disassociate union with Christ from that life. Rather, by performing their work according to God's will they can grow in that union. In this way must the laity make progress in holiness, showing a ready and happy spirit, and trying prudently and patiently to overcome difficulties. Neither family concerns nor other secular affairs' should be excluded from their religious program of life. For as the apostle states, "Whatever you do in word or work, do all in the name of the Lord Jesus Christ, giving thanks to God the Father through him" (Col. 3:17) (DAL, N. 4).

2.

Wishing to intensify the apostolic activity of the People of God, this most holy Synod earnestly addresses itself to the laity, whose proper and indispensable role in the mission of the Church it has already called to mind in other documents. The layman's apostolate derives from his Christian vocation, and the Church can never be without it. Sacred Scripture clearly shows how spontaneous and fruitful such activity was at the very beginning of the Church (cf. Acts 11:19-21; 18:26; Rom. 16:1-16; Phil. 4:3) (DAL, N. 1).

Description of Apostolate

3.
The term laity is here understood to mean all the faithful except those in Holy Orders and those in a religious state sanctioned by the Church. These faithful are by Baptism made one body with Christ and are established among the People of God. They are in their own way made sharers in the priestly, prophetic, and kingly functions of Christ. They carry out in their own particular way the mission of the whole Christian people with respect to the Church and the world (DCC, N. 31).

4.
For this the Church was founded: that by spreading the kingdom of Christ everywhere for the glory of God the Father, she might bring all men to share in Christ's saving redemption; and that through them the whole world might be in actual fact brought into relationship with Him. All activity of the Mystical Body directed to the attainment of this goal is called the apostolate, and the Church carries it on in various ways through all her members. For by its very nature the Christian vocation is also a vocation to the apostolate. No part of the structure of a living body is merely passive but each has a share in the functions as well as in the life of the body. So, too, in the Body of Christ, which is the Church, the whole Body, "according to the functioning in due measure of

each single part, derives its increase'' (Eph. 4:16). Indeed, so intimately are the parts linked and interrelated in this Body (cf. Eph. 4:16) that the member who fails to make his proper contribution to the development of the Church must be said to be useful neither to the Church nor to himself (DAL, N. 2).

5.
The laity derive the right and duty with respect to the apostolate from their union with Christ the head. Incorporated into Christ's Mystical Body through Baptism and strengthened by the power of the Holy Spirit through Confirmation, they are assigned to the apostolate by the Lord himself. They are consecrated into a royal priesthood and a holy people (cf. 1 Peter 2:4-10) in order that they may offer spiritual sacrifices through everything they do, and may witness to Christ throughout the world. For their part, the sacraments, especially the most Holy Eucharist, communicate and nourish that charity which is the soul of the entire apostolate (DAL, N. 3).

6.
The lay apostolate, however, is a participation in the saving mission of the Church itself. Through their Baptism and Confirmation, all are commissioned to that apostolate by the Lord himself. Moreover, through the sacraments, especially the Holy Eucharist, there is communicated and nourished that charity toward God and man which is the soul of the entire apostolate. Now, the laity are called in a special way to make the Church present and operative in those places and circumstances where only through them can she become the salt of the earth. Thus every layman, by virtue of the very gifts bestowed upon him, is at the same

time a witness and a living instrument of the mission of the Church herself, "according to the measure of Christ's bestowal" (Eph. 4:7) (DCC, N. 33).

Individual Apostolate

7.

The laity can engage in their apostolic activity either as individuals or as members of various groups or associations. The individual apostolate, flowing generously from the wellspring of a truly Christian life (cf. John 4:14), is the origin and condition of the whole lay apostolate, even in its organized expression, and admits of no substitute. Regardless of circumstance, all lay persons (including those who have no opportunity or possibility for collaboration in associations) are called to this type of apostolate and obliged to engage in it. Such an apostolate is useful at all times and places, but in certain circumstances it is the only one appropriate and feasible (DAL, N. 15, 16).

8.

The individual apostolate has an area of special opportunity wherever Catholics are few in number and widely dispersed. Here the laity who engage in the apostolate only as individuals, whether for the reasons already mentioned or for special reasons including those deriving from their own professional activity, can still usefully gather into small discussion groups lacking the more formal kind of establishment or organization. In this way an indication of the community of the Church can always be apparent to others as a true witness of love. Moreover, by giving spiritual help to one another through friendship and the sharing of experiences, they gain strength to overcome the disadvantages of an excessively isolated life and activity, and to make their apostolate more productive (DAL, N. 17).

9.
There are many forms of the apostolate in which the laity build up the Church, sanctify the world, and give it life in Christ. A particular form of the individual apostolate, as well as a sign especially suited for our times, is the testimony of a layman's entire life as it develops out of faith, hope, and charity. This form manifests Christ living in those who believe in Him. Then by the apostolate of the word, which is utterly necessary under certain circumstances, lay people announce Christ, explain and spread His teaching according to their situation and ability, and faithfully profess it (DAL, N. 16).

10.
There is a very urgent need for this individual apostolate in places where the freedom of the Church is seriously restricted. In exceedingly trying circumstances, the laity do what they can to take the place of priests, risking their freedom and sometimes their lives to teach Christian doctrine to those around them, to train them in a religious way of life and to engage in it. Such an apostolate is useful at all times and places, but in certain circumstances it is the only one appropriate and feasible. There are many forms of the apostolate in which the laity build up the Church, sanctify the world, and give it life in Christ (DAL, N. 17).

11.
The layman's religious program of life should take its special quality from his status as a married man

and a family man, or as one who is unmarried or widowed, from his state of health, and from his professional and social activity. He should not cease to develop earnestly the qualities and talents bestowed on him in accord with these conditions of life, and he should make use of the gifts which he has received from the Holy Spirit (DAL, N. 4).

12.
Since laymen share in their own way in the mission of the Church, their apostolic formation takes its special flavor from the distinctively secular quality of the lay state and from its own form of spirituality (DAL, N. 29).

Formation for Individual Apostolate

13.
Formation for the apostolate means a certain human and well-rounded formation adapted to the natural abilities and circumstances of each lay person. Well informed about the modern world, the lay person should be an active member of his own society and be adjusted to its culture (DAL, N. 29).

14.
The apostolate can attain maximum effectiveness only through a diversified and thorough formation. Such training is demanded not only by the continuous spiritual and doctrinal progress of the lay person himself but also by the need to adapt his activity to circumstances which vary according to the affairs, persons, and duties involved. This formation for the apostolate should rest upon those fundamentals which have been defended and proclaimed by this most holy Council in other documents. In addition to the formation which is

common for all Christians, many forms of the apostolate require a specific and particular formation as well, because of the variety of persons and circumstances (DAL, N. 28).

15.
Since formation for the apostolate cannot consist in merely theoretical instruction, from the very beginning of their formation, the laity should gradually and prudently learn how to view, judge, and do all things in the light of faith as well as to develop and improve themselves and others through action, thereby entering into the energetic service of the Church. This formation, always in need of improvement because of the increasing maturity of the human person and the unfolding of problems, requires an ever deeper knowledge and the adjustment of activities. In the fulfillment of all the demands of formation, the unity and integrity of the human personality must be kept in mind at all times, so that its harmony and balance may be safeguarded and enhanced (DAL, N. 29).

16.
Above all, however, the lay person should learn to advance the mission of Christ and the Church by basing his life on belief in the divine mystery of creation and redemption, and by being sensitive to the movement of the Holy Spirit, who gives life to the People of God and who would impel all men to love God the Father as well as the world and mankind in Him. This formation should be deemed the basis and condition for every successful apostolate (DAL, N. 29).

17.
In addition to spiritual formation, there is needed solid doctrinal instruction in theology, ethics, and

philosophy, instruction adjusted to differences of age, status, and natural talents. The importance of acquiring general culture along with practical and technical training should not be overlooked in the least (DAL, N. 29).

18.
For the cultivation of good human relations, truly human values must be fostered, especially the art of living fraternally with others, cooperating with them, and initiating conversation with them (DAL, N. 29).

19.
There already exist many aids for lay persons devoted to the apostolate, namely, study sessions, congresses, periods of recollection, spiritual exercises, frequent meetings, conferences, books, and periodicals. All these are directed toward the acquisition of a deeper knowledge of Sacred Scripture and Catholic doctrine, the nourishment of spiritual life, an appreciation of world conditions, and the discovery and development of suitable methods. These formative aids take into account the various types of the apostolate, according to the milieu in which it is to be exercised. For this purpose, too, centers or advanced institutes have been erected, and have already proved highly successful (DAL, N. 32).

Education as Means of Formation

20.
Training for the apostolate should start with a child's earliest education. In a special way, however, adolescents and young adults should be initiated into the apostolate and imbued with its spirit. This formation must be perfected through-

out their whole lives in keeping with the demands of new responsibilities. It is evident, therefore, that those who have the obligation to provide Christian education also have the duty to provide for formation in the apostolate (DAL, N. 30).

21.

Children must also be educated to transcend the family circle, and to open their minds to ecclesiastical and temporal communities. They should be so involved in the local community of the parish that they will acquire a consciousness of being living and active members of the People of God. In their catechetical instructions, their ministry of the Word, their direction of souls, and in their other parish and pastoral services, priests should be preoccupied with forming apostles (DAL, N. 30).

22.

Schools, colleges, and other Catholic educational institutions also have the duty to develop a Catholic sense and apostolic activity in young people. If young people lack this formation either because they do not attend these schools or because of any other reason, parents, pastors of souls, and apostolic organizations should attend to it all the more. Teachers and educators, who carry on a distinguished form of the apostolate of the laity by their vocation and office, should be equipped with the learning and pedagogical skill needed for imparting such apostolic training effectively (DAL, N. 30).

Hierarchy and Individual Apostolate

23.

The hierarchy should promote the apostolate of the laity, provide it with spiritual principles and support, direct the exercise of this apostolate to the common good of the Church, and attend to the preservation of doctrine and order. Depending on its various forms and goals, the lay apostolate admits of different types of relationships with the hierarchy (DAL, N. 24).

24.
For in the Church there are many apostolic undertakings which are established by the free choice of the laity and regulated by their prudent judgment. The mission of the Church can be better accomplished in certain circumstances by undertakings of this kind, and therefore they are frequently praised or recommended by the hierarchy. No project, however, may claim the name "Catholic" unless it has obtained the consent of the lawful Church authority. Certain forms of the apostolate of the laity are given explicit recognition by the hierarchy, though in various ways (DAL, N. 24).

25.
Bishops, pastors of parishes, and other priests of both branches of the clergy should keep in mind that the right and duty to exercise the apostolate is common to all the faithful, both clergy and laity, and that the laity also have their own proper roles in building up the Church. For this reason, they should work fraternally with the laity in and for the Church and take special care of the lay persons engaged in apostolic works (DAL, N. 25).

26.
The pastors of the Church should gladly and gratefully welcome these lay persons and make sure that their situation meets the demands of justice, equity, and charity to the fullest possible extent, particularly as regards proper support for them and their families. Pastors should also see to it that

these lay people enjoy the necessary formation, spiritual consolation, and incentive (DAL, N. 22).

27.
In this way the lay person will throw himself wholly and energetically into the reality of the temporal order and effectively assume his role in conducting its affairs. At the same time, as a living member and witness of the Church, he will make the Church present and active in the midst of temporal affairs (DAL, N. 29).

Christ as Focal Point
28.
The Church also keeps in mind the advice of the apostle, who summoned the faithful to charity by exhorting them to share the mind of Christ Jesus — He who "emptied himself, taking the nature of a slave . . . becoming obedient to death" (Phil. 2:7, 8), and, because of us, "being rich, he became poor" (2 Cor. 8:9) (DCC, N. 42).

29.
Such a life requires a continual exercise of faith, hope, and charity. Only by the light of faith and by meditation on the Word of God can one always and everywhere recognize God in whom "we live, and move, and have our being" (Acts 17:28), seek His will in every event, see Christ in all men whether they be close to us or strangers, and make correct judgments about the true meaning and value of temporal things, both in themselves and in their relation to man's final goal (DAL, N. 4).

Mary as Prototype
30.
The perfect example of this type of spiritual and apostolic life is the most Blessed Virgin Mary,

Queen of the Apostles. While leading a life on earth common to all men, one filled with family concerns and labors, she was always intimately united with her Son and cooperated in the work of the Savior in a manner altogether special. Now that she has been taken up into heaven, "with her maternal charity she cares for these brothers of her Son who are still on their earthly pilgrimage and are surrounded by dangers and difficulties; she will care until they are led into their blessed fatherland" (*Dogmatic Constitution on the Church*, N. 62). All should devoutly venerate her and commend their life and apostolate to her motherly concern (DAL, N. 4).

POINTS TO PONDER

Why is the lay apostolate dependent upon union with Christ? (1 and 2)

What is the apostolate of the laity? (3 through 6)

What is the individual apostolate? (7 through 12)

What formation does this apostolate require? (13 through 22)

What relationship exists between the hierarchy and lay apostles? (23 through 27)

Why are lay people expected to be always apostolic? (28 through 30)

MAY: ORGANIZED APOSTOLATE

SYNOPSIS

The laity are members of Christ's Body: "a chosen race, a royal priesthood, a holy nation, a purchased people." They are God's instrument for the salvation of the world, a seed of hope, a source of unity, a cause of redemption for all mankind.

Apostolic organizations greatly aid the Church in her mission. While all laymen must carry on an individual apostolate, still man is social by nature and the group type of apostolate corresponds to a deep human need. Besides, institutions of society are influenced and changed primarily through concerted action.

The twofold aim of lay apostolic organizations is to make the Gospel known and lead men to holiness by programs of action which are their responsibility, but under the direction of the hierarchy. Church authority can mandate apostolic associations for some particular responsibility, but in doing so, the integrity of the associations must be respected and preserved.

Councils which include members of the apostolic organizations should be established on the diocesan, national and international levels to assure the attainment of common goals and the avoidance of destructive rivalries.

Lay people need proper formation in order to take part effectively in the organized apostolate. Spiritual formation is not enough; they must receive adequate preparation in all aspects of life needed to accomplish their task. Here, too, Mary is the archetype.

DEVELOPMENT

Christ formed a Messianic people to carry on His work (1 through 4).

The Church needs apostolic organizations (5 and 6).

Laymen are called to the organized apostolate (7 through 9).

This type of apostolate offers much variety (10 through 12).

Laymen have responded generously to this need (13 through 16).

All forms of the organized apostolate must be respected (17 through 20).

Councils should be established to coordinate the work (21 through 24).

Laymen must be properly formed for the group apostolate (25 through 28).

A mature laity is required (29 and 30).

Mary is the exemplar (31).

MAY
ORGANIZED APOSTOLATE

Christ Formed a Messianic People

1.

In the human nature which He united to himself, the Son of God redeemed man and transformed him into a new creation (cf. Gal. 6:15; 2 Cor. 5:17) by overcoming death through His own death and Resurrection. By communicating His Spirit to His brothers, called together from all peoples, Christ made them mystically into His own body (DCC, N. 7).

2.

This was to be the new People of God. For, those who believe in Christ, who are reborn not from a perishable but from an imperishable seed through the Word of the living God (cf. 1 Peter, 1:23), not from the flesh but from water and the Holy Spirit (cf. John 3:5-6), are finally established as "a chosen race, a royal priesthood, a holy nation, a purchased people . . . You who in times past were not a people, but are now the People of God" (1 Peter 2:9-10) (DCC, N. 9).

3.

That Messianic people has for its head Christ, "who was delivered up for our sins, and rose again for our justification" (Rom. 4:25), and who now, having won a name which is above all names, reigns in glory in heaven. The heritage of this people are the dignity and freedom of the sons of God, in whose hearts the Holy Spirit dwells as in His temple. Its law is the new commandment to

love as Christ loved us (cf. John 13:34). Its goal is
the kingdom of God, which has been begun by
God himself on earth, and which is to be further
extended until it is brought to perfection by Him
at the end of time. Then Christ our life (cf. Col.
3:4) will appear, and "creation itself also will be
delivered from its slavery to corruption into the
freedom of the glory of the sons of God" (Rom.
8:21) (DCC, N. 9).

4.
So it is that this Messianic people, although it does
not actually include all men, and may more than
once look like a small flock, is nonetheless a lasting and sure seed of unity, hope, and salvation for
the whole human race. Established by Christ as a
fellowship of life, charity, and truth, it is also used
by Him as an instrument for the redemption of all,
and is sent forth into the whole world as the light
of the world and the salt of the earth (cf. Matt.
5:13-16) (DDC, N. 9).

Church Needs Apostolic Organizations

5.
The Church derives great joy from the fact that
every day an increasing number of lay persons
offer their personal service to apostolic associations
and activities, either within the limits of their own
nation or in the international field, or especially in
Catholic mission communities and in regions
where the Church has only recently been implanted (DAL, N. 22).

6.
Whether the lay apostolate is exercised by the
faithful as individuals or as members of organizations, it should be incorporated into the aposto-

late of the whole Church according to a right system of relationships. Indeed, union with those whom the Holy Spirit has assigned to rule God's Church (cf. Acts 20:28) is an essential element of the Christian apostolate. No less necessary is cooperation among the various projects of the apostolate, which have to be suitably coordinated by the hierarchy (DAL, N. 23).

Call to the Organized Apostolate

7.
The faithful are called upon to engage in the apostolate as individuals in the varying circumstances of their life. They should remember, nevertheless, that man is naturally social and that it has pleased God to unite those who believe in Christ in the People of God (cf. 1 Peter 2:5-10) and into one body (cf. 1 Cor. 12:12). Hence the group apostolate of Christian believers happily corresponds to a human and Christian need and at the same time signifies the communion and unity of the Church in Christ, who said, "Where two or three are gathered together for my sake, there am I in the midst of them" (Matt. 18:20) (DAL, N. 18).

8.
The faithful should be vigorously urged to assume their duty of carrying on the apostolate, each according to his state of life and his ability. They should be invited to join or assist the various works of the lay apostolate, especially Catholic Action. Those associations should be promoted also and supported which either directly or indirectly pursue a supernatural goal, for example, attaining a saintlier life, spreading the Gospel of Christ to all men, promoting Christian doctrine or the liturgical apostolate, pursuing social aims, or

performing works of piety and charity (DBPOC, N. 17).

9.
For this reason the faithful should exercise their apostolate by way of united effort. Let them be apostles both in their family communities and in their parishes and dioceses, which themselves express the community nature of the apostolate, as well as in voluntary groups which they decide to join. The group apostolate is highly important also because the apostolate must often be implemented through joint action, in both the church communities and various other spheres. For the associations established to carry on the apostolate in common sustain their members, form them in the apostolate, and rightly organize and regulate their apostolic work so that much better results can be expected than if each member were to act on his own (DAL, N. 18).

Variety of Apostolates

10.
There are a great variety of associations in the apostolate. Some set before themselves the broad apostolic purpose of the Church; others aim to evangelize and sanctify in a special way. Some propose to infuse a Christian spirit into the temporal order. Others bear witness to Christ in a particular way through works of mercy and charity (DAL, N. 19).

11.
In the present circumstances, it is quite necessary that, in the area of lay activity, the united and organized form of the apostolate be strengthened. In fact, only the close pooling of resources is

capable of fully achieving all the aims of the modern apostolate and firmly protecting its interests. Here it is especially important that the apostolate concern itself too with the common attitudes and social background of those members for whom it is designed. Otherwise, those engaged in the apostolate will often be unequal to the pressure of public opinion or of social institutions (DAL, N. 18).

12.
Among these associations, those which promote and encourage a closer harmony between the everyday life of the members and their faith must be given primary consideration. Associations are not ends unto themselves; rather they should serve to fulfill the Church's mission to the world. Their apostolic dynamism depends upon their conformity with the goals of the Church as well as on the Christian witness and evangelical spirit of the individual member and of the association as a whole (DAL, N. 19).

Need Responded to Generously
13.
As long as the proper relationship is kept to Church authorities, the laity have the right to found and run such associations and to join those already existing. Yet the scattering of energies must be avoided. This waste occurs when new associations and projects are promoted without a sufficient reason, or if antiquated associations or methods are retained beyond their period of usefulness. Nor is it always fitting to make an indiscriminate transfer to other nations of forms of the apostolate that have been used in one nation (DAL, N. 19).

14.

More than a few decades ago the laity in many nations began to dedicate themselves increasingly to the apostolate. They grouped themselves into various kinds of activities and societies which, in rather close union with the hierarchy, pursued and continue to pursue goals which are properly apostolic. Among these associations, or even among similar but older ones, those are especially noteworthy which followed different methods of operation and yet produced excellent results for Christ's kingdom, and were deservedly recommended and promoted by the popes and many bishops. From these they received the title of "Catholic Action." This was very often described as involving the collaboration of the laity in the apostolate of the hierarchy (DAL, N. 20).

15.

Whether these forms of the apostolate have the name of "Catholic Action" or some other title they exercise an apostolate of great value for our times and are composed of the combined and simultaneous possession of the following characteristics: a) The immediate aim of organizations of this kind is the Church's apostolic aim, that is, to make the Gospel known and men holy, and to form in them a Christian conscience so that they can infuse the spirit of the Gospel into the various communities and spheres of life. b) Cooperating with the hierarchy in their own way, the laity contribute the benefit of their experience to the running of these organizations, to the weighing of the conditions in which the pastoral activity of the Church has to be conducted, and to the hammering out and carrying out of a program of action. In all such matters, they assume responsibility (DAL, N. 20).

16.
c) The laity act together in the manner of an organic body so that the community nature of the Church is more fittingly symbolized and the apostolate rendered more effective. d) Whether they offer themselves spontaneously or are invited to act and to cooperate directly with the apostolate of the hierarchy, the laity function under the higher direction of the hierarchy itself, and the latter can sanction this cooperation by an explicit mandate. Organizations in which, in the opinion of the hierarchy, the ensemble of these characteristics is realized, must be considered to be Catholic Action even though they take on various forms and titles because of the needs of the different regions and peoples (DAL, N. 20).

Respect Demanded for All Forms

17.
All associations of the apostolate must be given due appreciation. Those, however, which the hierarchy has praised or recommended as responsive to the needs of time and place, or has directed to be established as particularly urgent, must be held in highest esteem by priests, religious, and laity and promoted according to each one's ability. Among these associations, moreover, international associations or groups of Catholics must be especially prized today (DAL, N. 21).

18.
Deserving of special honor and commendation in the Church are those lay people, single or married,

who devote themselves and their professional skill either permanently or temporarily, to the service of associations and their activities (DAL, No. 22).

19.

Because of the demands of the common good of the Church, moreover, ecclesiastical authority can select and promote in a particular way some of the apostolic associations and projects which have an immediately spiritual purpose, thereby assuming in them a special responsibility. Thus, making various dispositions of the apostolate according to circumstances, the hierarchy joins some particular form of it more closely with its own apostolic function. Yet the proper nature and individuality of each apostolate must be preserved, and the laity must not be deprived of the possibility of acting on their own accord. In various Church documents, this procedure of the hierarchy is called a mandate (DAL, N. 24).

20.

Finally, the hierarchy entrusts to the laity some functions which are more closely connected with pastoral duties, such as the teaching of Christian doctrine, certain liturgical actions, and the care of souls. By virtue of this mission, the laity are fully subject to higher ecclesiastical direction in the performance of such work (DAL, N. 24).

Councils Needed for Coordination
21.

In dioceses, as far as possible, there should be councils which assist the apostolic work of the Church either in the field of making the Gospel known and men holy, or in the charitable, social, or other spheres. To this end, clergy and religious should appropriately cooperate with the laity. While preserving the proper character and autonomy of each organization, these councils will be able to promote the mutual coordination of various lay associations and enterprises. Councils of this type should be established as far as possible also on the parochial, interparochial, and interdiocesan level as well as in the national and international sphere (DAL, N. 26).

22.

Various forms of the apostolate should be encouraged, and in the whole diocese or in given areas of it the coordination and close interconnection of all apostolic works should be fostered under the direction of the bishop. In this way, all undertakings and organizations, whether catechetical, missionary, charitable, social, family, educational, or any other program serving a pastoral goal, will be brought into harmonious action. At the same time the unity of the diocese will thereby be made more evident (DBPOC, N. 17).

23.

Some special secretariat, moreover, should be established at the Holy See for the service and encouragement of the lay apostolate. It can serve as a center well equipped for communicating information about the various apostolic programs of the laity, promoting research into modern problems arising in this field, and assisting with its advice the hierarchy and laity in their apostolic works. The various movements and projects of the apostolate of the laity throughout the world should also be represented in this secretariat, and here clergy and religious also are to cooperate with the laity (DAL, N. 26).

24.

Indeed, if the spirit of unity is to be promoted so that fraternal charity may be resplendent in the whole apostolate of the Church, common goals attained, and destructive rivalries avoided, there must exist mutual esteem between all forms of the apostolate in the Church and, with due respect for the particular character of each organization, proper coordination. Such esteem and coordination are most fitting, since any particular activity in the Church requires harmony and apostolic cooperation on the part of both branches of the clergy, as well as the religious, and the laity (DAL, N. 23).

Formation of Laymen Necessary

25.

In keeping with their purpose and according to their measure, lay groups and associations dedicated to the apostolate or to other supernatural goals should carefully and persistently promote formation for the apostolate. Frequently these groups are the ordinary vehicle of harmonious formation for the apostolate since they provide doctrinal, spiritual, and practical formation. Their members meet in small groups with their associates or friends, examine the methods and results of their apostolic activity, and measure their daily way of life against the Gospel (DAL, N. 30).

26.

Formation of this type must be designed to take into account the whole lay apostolate, which is to be carried on not only among the organized groups themselves but also in all circumstances of a man's life, especially his professional and social life. Indeed, everyone should painstakingly ready himself personally for the apostolate, especially as an adult. For the advance of age brings with it better self-knowledge, thus enabling each person to evaluate more accurately the talents with which God has enriched his soul and to exercise more effectively those charismatic gifts which the Holy Spirit has bestowed on him for the good of his brothers (DAL, N. 30).

27.
Since the words of charity and mercy afford the most striking testimony of the Christian life, apostolic formation should lead also to the performance of these works so that the faithful may learn from childhood to have compassion for their brothers and to be generous in helping those in need (DAL, N. 31).

28.
Furthermore, the laity who in pursuit of their vocation have become members of one of the associations or institutes approved by the Church are trying faithfully to adopt the special characteristics of the spiritual life which are proper to these as well. They should also hold in high esteem professional skill, family and civic spirit, and the virtues relating to social behavior, namely, honesty, justice, sincerity, kindness, and courage, without which there can be no true Christian life (DAL, N. 4).

Mature Laity Required

29.
The Church has not yet been fully established, and is not yet fully alive, nor is it a perfect sign of Christ among men, unless there exists a laity worthy of the name working along with the hierarchy.

For the Gospel cannot be deeply imprinted on the talents, life, and work of any people without the active presence of laymen. Therefore, even in the very founding of a Church, the greatest attention is to be paid to the raising up of a mature Christian laity (DCMA, N. 21).

30.

Finally, the laity should vivify their lives with charity and express it as best they can in their works. Let each one remember that he can have an impact on all men and contribute to the salvation of the whole world by public worship and prayer as well as by penance and voluntary acceptance of the labors and hardships of life. By such means does the Christian grow in likeness to the suffering Christ (cf. 2 Cor. 4:10; Col. 1:24) (DAL, N. 16).

Mary the Exemplar

31.

For Mary figured profoundly in the history of salvation and in a certain way unites and mirrors within herself the central truths of the faith. Hence when she is being preached and venerated, she summons the faithful to her Son and His sacrifice, and to love for the Father. Seeking after the glory of Christ, the Church becomes more like her exalted model, and continually progresses in faith, hope, and charity, searching out and doing the will of God in all things. Hence the Church in her apostolic work also rightly looks to her who brought forth Christ, conceived by the Holy Spirit and born of the Virgin, so that through the Church Christ may be born and grow in the hearts of the faithful also. The Virgin Mary in her own life lived an example of that maternal love by which all should be fittingly animated who cooperate in the apostolic mission of the Church on behalf of the rebirth of men (DCC, N. 65).

POINTS TO PONDER

What does Christ expect of His purchased people? (1 through 4)

Why are laymen needed in organized apostolic work? (5 through 12)

How are apostolic associations related to the hierarchy? (13 through 20)

Why coordinate the work of such organizations? (21 through 24)

Do laymen need formation for the group apostolate? (25 through 28)

What is the goal of the organized apostolate? (29 through 31)

JUNE: CHRISTIAN HUMANISTS

SYNOPSIS

God has created all men to form a single people. Christ founded a brotherly community and sanctified all of the ties which bind men together. Today in every nation there are men and women who are conscious that they themselves are the artisans of culture on the national and international levels.

A new humanism is being born as men recognize their responsibility toward their brothers and history itself. Modern improvements in communications are contributing to the development of a more universal form of culture which can further promote the unity of mankind. At the same time, reverence for man and his rights is growing. Every man is a neighbor with personal dignity and human rights. Therefore whatever is opposed to human life is infamous.

The institutions of society must promote all that is humanly best for man. Nothing will better achieve this than Christian education which is designed to develop the finest aspects of the human spirit.

Although differences exist between men, respect and love ought to be extended to all as they work together, contributing their efforts to the realization of God's plan for the perfection of the whole of creation. In this way the triumphs of the human race will be signs of God's greatness and the flowering of His mysterious design.

Thus the goal of all human activity is to allow men to pursue their total vocation and fulfill it.

DEVELOPMENT

God has created men to form a brotherly community (1 through 4).

Men are becoming more conscious of their universal brotherhood (5 and 6).

Every man has personal dignity and human rights (7 through 13).

Education contributes significantly to cultural growth (14 through 17).

All men are worthy of respect and love (18 through 20).

Humanization is an ongoing process (21 through 28).

The goal of all human activity (29 and 30).

JUNE

CHRISTIAN HUMANISTS

A Brotherly Community

1.

God did not create man for life in isolation, but for the formation of social unity. So also "it has pleased God to make men holy and save them not merely as individuals, without any mutual bonds, but by making them into a single people, a people which acknowledges Him in truth and serves Him in holiness" (*Dogmatic Constitution on the Church*, N. 9). So from the beginning of salvation history He has chosen men not just as individuals, but as members of a certain community. Revealing His mind to them, God called these chosen ones "his people" (Ex. 3:7-12), and furthermore made a covenant with them on Sinai (CCMW, N. 32).

2.

As the first-born of many brethren and through the gift of His Spirit, Christ founded after His death and Resurrection a new brotherly community composed of all those who receive Him in faith and love. This He did through His Body, which is the Church. There everyone, as members one of the other, would render mutual service according to the different gifts bestowed on each. This solidarity must be constantly increased until that day on which it will be brought to perfection. Then, saved by grace, men will offer flawless glory to God as a family beloved of God and of Christ their brother (CCMW, N. 32).

3.

In His preaching He clearly taught the sons of God to treat each other as brothers. In His prayers He pleaded that all His disciples might be "one." Indeed, as the redeemer of all, He offered himself for all even to the point of death. "Greater love than this no one has, that one lay down his life for his friends" (John 15:13). He commanded His disciples to preach to all peoples the Gospel message so that the human race might become the family of God, in which the fullness of the Law would be love (CCMW, N. 32).

4.
This communitarian character is developed and consummated in the work of Jesus Christ. For the very Word made flesh willed to share in the human fellowship. He was present at the wedding of Cana, visited the house of Zacchaeus, ate with publicans and sinners. He revealed the love of the Father and the sublime vocation of man in terms of the most common of social realities and by making use of the speech and imagery of plain everyday life. Willingly obeying the laws of his country, He sanctified those human ties, especially family ones, from which social relationships arise. He chose to lead the life proper to an artisan of His time and place (CCMW, N. 32).

Universal Brotherhood

5.
In every group and nation, there is an ever-increasing number of men and women who are conscious that they themselves are the artisans and the authors of the culture of their community. Throughout the world there is a similar growth in the combined sense of independence and responsibility. Such a development is of paramount importance for the spiritual and moral maturity of the human race. This truth grows clearer if we

consider how the world is becoming unified and how we have the duty to build a better world based upon truth and justice. Thus we are witnesses of the birth of a new humanism, one in which man is defined first of all by his responsibility toward his brothers and toward history (CCMW, N. 55).

6.

Hence the culture of today possesses particular characteristics. For example, the so-called exact sciences sharpen critical judgment to a very fine edge. Recent psychological research explains human activity more profoundly. Historical studies make a signal contribution to bringing men to see things in their changeable and evolutionary aspects. Customs and usages are becoming increasingly uniform. Industrialization, urbanization, and other causes of community living create new forms of culture (mass culture), from which arise many new ways of thinking, acting, and making use of leisure. The growth of communications between the various nations and social groups opens more widely to all the treasures of different cultures. Thus, little by little, a more universal form of human culture is developing, one which will promote and express the unity of the human race to the degree that it preserves the particular features of the different cultures (CCMW, N. 54).

Personal Dignity and Human Rights

7.

At the same time, however, there is a growing awareness of the exalted dignity proper to the human person, since he stands above all things, and his rights and duties are universal and inviolable. Therefore, there must be made available to all men everything necessary for leading a life truly human, such as food, clothing, and shelter; the right to choose a state of life freely and to found a family, the right to education, to employment, to a good reputation, to respect, to appropriate information, to activity in accord with the upright norm of one's own conscience, to protection of privacy and to rightful freedom in matters religious too (CCMW, N. 26).

8.
Coming down to the practical and particularly urgent consequences, this Council lays stress on reverence for man; everyone must consider his every neighbor without exception as another self, taking into account first of all his life and the means necessary to living it with dignity, so as not to imitate the rich man who had no concern for the poor man Lazarus (CCMW, N. 27).

9.
In our times a special obligation binds us to make ourselves the neighbor of absolutely every person, and of actively helping him when he comes across our path, whether he be an old person abandoned by all, a foreign laborer unjustly looked down upon, a refugee, a child born of an unlawful union and wrongly suffering for a sin he did not commit, or a hungry person who disturbs our conscience by recalling the voice of the Lord: "As long as you did it for one of these, the least of my brethren, you did it for me" (Matt. 25:40) (CCMW, N. 27).

10.
Furthermore, whatever is opposed to life itself, such as any type of murder, genocide, abortion, euthanasia, or willful destruction, whatever violates the integrity of the human person such as

mutilation, torments inflicted upon body or mind, attempts to coerce the will itself; whatever insults human dignity, such as subhuman living conditions, arbitrary imprisonment, deportation, slavery, prostitution, the selling of women and children; as well as disgraceful working conditions, where men are treated as mere tools for profit, rather than as free and responsible persons; all these things and others of their like are infamies indeed. They poison human society, but they do more harm to those who practice them than those who suffer from the injury. Moreover, they are a supreme dishonor to the creator (CCMW, N. 27).

11.
True, all men are not alike from the point of view of varying physical power and the diversity of intellectual and moral resources. Nevertheless, with respect to the fundamental rights of the person, every type of discrimination, whether social or cultural, whether based on sex, race, color, social condition, language, or religion, is to be overcome and eradicated as contrary to God's intent. For in truth it must still be regretted that fundamental personal rights are not yet universally honored. Such is the case of a woman who is denied the right and freedom to choose a husband, to embrace a state of life, or to acquire an education or cultural benefits equal to those recognized for men (CCMW, N. 29).

12.
Human institutions, both private and public, must labor to minister to the dignity and purpose of man. At the same time let them put up a stubborn fight against any kind of slavery, whether social or political, and safeguard the basic rights of man

under every political system. Indeed human institutions themselves must be accommodated by degrees to the highest of all realities, spiritual ones, even though meanwhile, a long enough time will be required before they arrive at the desired goal (CCMW, N. 29).

13.
Moreover, although rightful differences exist between men, the equal dignity of persons demands that a more humane and just condition of life be brought about. For excessive economic and social differences between the members of the one human family or population groups cause scandal, and militate against social justice, equity, the dignity of the human person, as well as social and international peace (CCMW, N. 29).

Education Contributes to Culture

14.
In order for individual men to discharge with greater exactness the obligations of their conscience toward themselves and the various groups to which they belong, they must be carefully educated to a higher degree of culture through the use of the immense resources available today to the human race. Above all the education of youth from every social background has to be undertaken, so that there can be produced not only men and women of refined talents, but those great-souled persons who are so desperately required by our times (CCMW, N. 31).

15.
Since every Christian has become a new creature, by rebirth from water and the Holy Spirit, so that

he may be called what he truly is, a child of God, he is entitled to a Christian education. Such an education does not merely strive to foster in the human person the maturity already described. Rather, its principal aims are these: that as the baptized person is gradually introduced into a knowledge of the mystery of salvation, he may daily grow more conscious of the gift of faith which he has received; that he may learn to adore God the Father in spirit and in truth (cf. John 4:23), especially through liturgical worship; that he may be trained to conduct his personal life in righteousness and in the sanctity of truth, according to his new standard of manhood (Eph. 4:22-24) (DCE, N. 2).

16.

Today it is more difficult than ever for a synthesis to be formed of the various branches of knowledge and the arts. For while the mass and the diversity of cultural factors are increasing, there is a decline in the individual man's ability to grasp and unify these elements. Thus the ideal of the "universal man" is disappearing more and more. Nevertheless, it remains each man's duty to preserve a view of the whole human person, a view in which the values of intellect, will, conscience, and fraternity are preeminent. These values are all rooted in God the creator and have been wonderfully restored and elevated in Christ (CCMW, N. 61).

17.

Since every man of whatever race, condition, and age is endowed with the dignity of a person, he has an inalienable right to an education corresponding to his proper destiny and suited to his native talents, his sex, his cultural background, and his ancestral heritage. At the same time, this education should pave the way for brotherly association with other peoples, so that genuine unity and peace on earth may be promoted. For a true education aims at the formation of the human person with respect to his ultimate goal, and simultaneously with respect to the good of those societies of which, as a man, he is a member, and in whose responsibilities, as an adult, he will share (DCE, N. 1).

All Deserve Respect and Love

18.

Respect and love ought to be extended also to those who think or act differently than we do in social, political, and religious matters, too. In fact, the more deeply we come to understand their ways of thinking through such courtesy and love, the more easily will we be able to enter into dialogue with them (CCMW, N. 28).

19.

This love and good will, to be sure, must in no way render us indifferent to truth and goodness. Indeed love itself impels the disciples of Christ to speak the saving truth to all men. But it is necessary to distinguish between error, which always merits repudiation, and the person in error, who never loses the dignity of being a person, even when he is flawed by some false or inadequate religious notions. God alone is the judge and searcher of hearts; for that reason He forbids us to make judgments about the internal guilt of anyone (CCMW, N. 28).

20.

Since all men possess a rational soul and are created in God's likeness, since they have the same nature and origin, have been redeemed by Christ, and enjoy the same divine calling and destiny, the basic equality of all must receive increasingly greater recognition (CCMW, N. 29).

Humanization an Ongoing Process

21.
Furthermore, when a man applies himself to the various disciplines of philosophy, of history, and of mathematical and natural science, and when he cultivates the arts, he can do very much to elevate the human family to a more sublime under-standing of truth, goodness, and beauty, and to the formation of judgments which embody univer-sal values. Thus mankind can more clearly be enlightened by that marvelous wisdom which was with God from all eternity, arranging all things with Him, playing upon the earth, delighting in the sons of men (CCMW, N. 57).

22.
In this way the human spirit grows increasingly free of its bondage to creatures and can be more easily drawn to the worship and contemplation of the creator. Moreover, under the impulse of grace, man is disposed to acknowledge the Word of God. He became flesh in order to save all things and sum them up in himself, "He was in the world" already as "the true light that enlightens every man" (John 1:9, 10) (CCMW, N. 57).

23.
Throughout the course of the centuries, men have labored to better the circumstances of their lives through a monumental amount of individual and collective effort. To believers, this point is settled: considered in itself, such human activity accords

with God's will. For man, created to God's image, received a mandate to subject to himself the earth and all that it contains, and to govern the world with justice and holiness; a mandate to relate himself and the totality of things to Him who was to be acknowledged as the Lord and creator of all. Thus, by the subjection of all things to man, the name of God would be wonderful in all the earth (CCMW, N. 34).

24.
This mandate concerns even the most ordinary everyday activities. For while providing the substance of life for themselves and their families, men and women are performing their activities in a way which appropriately benefits society. They can justly consider that by their labor they are unfolding the creator's work, consulting the advantages of their brother men, and contributing by their personal industry to the realization in history of the divine plan (CCMW, N. 34).

25.
Thus, far from thinking that works produced by man's own talent and energy are in opposition to God's power, and that the rational creature exists as a kind of rival to the creator, Christians are convinced that the triumphs of the human race are a sign of God's greatness and the flowering of His own mysterious design. For the greater man's power becomes, the farther his individual and community responsibility extends. Hence it is clear that men are not deterred by the Christian message from building up the world, or impelled to neglect the welfare of their brothers. They are, rather, more stringently bound to do these very things (CCMW, N. 34).

26.

Now a man can scarcely arrive at the needed sense of responsibility unless his living conditions allow him to become conscious of his dignity, and to rise to his destiny by spending himself for God and for others. But human freedom is often crippled when a man falls into extreme poverty, just as it withers when he indulges in too many of life's comforts and imprisons himself in a kind of splendid isolation. Freedom acquires new strength, by contrast, when a man consents to the unavoidable requirements of social life, takes on the manifold demands of human partnership, and commits himself to the service of the human community (CCMW, N. 31).

27.

Just as human activity proceeds from man, so it is ordered to man. For when a man works he not only alters things and society, he develops himself as well. He learns much, he cultivates his resources, he goes outside of himself and beyond himself. Rightly understood, this kind of growth is of greater value than any external riches which can be garnered. A man is more precious for what he is than for what he has. Similarly, all that men do to obtain greater justice, wider brotherhood, and a more humane offering of social relationships has greater worth than technical advances. For these advances can supply the material for human progress, but of themselves alone they can never actually bring it about (CCMW, N. 35).

28.

Human labor which is expended in the production and exchange of goods or in the performance of economic services is superior to the other elements of economic life. For the latter have only the nature of tools. Whether it is engaged in independently or paid for by someone else, this labor comes immediately from the person. In a sense, the person stamps the things of nature with his seal and subdues them to his will. It is ordinarily by his labor that a man supports himself and his family, is joined to his fellow-men and serves them, and is enabled to exercise genuine charity and be a partner in the work of bringing God's creation to perfection. Indeed, we hold that by offering his labor to God a man becomes associated with the redemptive work itself of Jesus Christ, who conferred an eminent quality on labor when at Nazareth He worked with His own hands (CCMW, N. 67).

Goal of All Human Activity

29.

For the aforementioned reasons, the Church recalls to the mind of all that culture must be made to bear on the integral perfection of the human person, and on the good of the community and the whole of society. Therefore the human spirit must be cultivated in such a way that there results a growth in its ability to develop a religious, moral, and social sense (CCMW, N. 59).

30.

Hence, the norm of human activity is this: that in accord with the divine plan and will, it should harmonize with the genuine good of the human race, and allow men as individuals and as members of society to pursue their total vocation and fulfill it (CCMW, N. 35).

POINTS TO PONDER

Why can Christ be called a true humanist? (1 through 4)

Why do human persons demand respect? (5 through 11)

How can social institutions minister to the purpose and dignity of man? (12 through 14)

What role can education play in developing the human person? (15 through 17)

What attitude should be assumed toward those who differ from us in their thoughts and attitudes? (18 through 20)

How free should men be in developing their human potentialities? (21 through 28)

What is the proper norm for all human activity? (29 and 30)

JULY:

BUILDERS OF THE TEMPORAL ORDER

SYNOPSIS

Christ has radically redeemed the whole temporal order, so the mission of the Church is to penetrate and perfect all of creation with the spirit of the Gospel. Laymen achieve this by letting the power of the Gospel regulate their lives in their families and in society. They build the kingdom of God by discharging their secular duties in an accountable Christian manner.

God's plan is that men should increasingly perfect the created order. In the temporal order, everything possesses its own intrinsic value and laymen have the task of sanctifying the entire world from within by developing it through the use of their talents under the guidance of faith. Laymen have duties to the Church and to the world; they can harmonize their allegiance to both by always acting according to the dictates of their conscience.

A secular quality is proper and special to laymen. When they improve this world and make it a better dwelling place for men, they are carrying out the intention of God to have the divine law govern the affairs of the earthly city. The apostolate of the social milieu — to infuse a Christian spirit into all elements of the community in which one lives — is so completely the duty of laymen that they alone can fulfill it. By united social action they can prepare the world for the seed of the Gospel.

Laymen must learn the true value of created things, live in close union with the men of their time and work with them to construct a more human world, while looking forward to that final day when all things will be transformed into the everlasting kingdom of God.

DEVELOPMENT

Christ redeems the temporal order through laymen (1 through 5).

Laymen are loyal citizens of two worlds (6 and 7).

The temporal order has its own proper value (8 and 9).

It is the responsibility of laymen to renew creation (10 through 14).

Secular life is the special domain of laymen (15 through 21).

The apostolate of the social milieu is indispensable (22 through 26).

The Church is working for the transformation of all things in Christ (27 through 31).

JULY
BUILDERS OF THE TEMPORAL ORDER

Christ Redeems through Laymen

1.

Christ's redemptive work, while of itself directed toward the salvation of men, involves also the renewal of the whole temporal order. Hence the mission of the Church is not only to bring to men the message and grace of Christ, but also to penetrate and perfect the temporal sphere with the spirit of the Gospel. In fulfilling this mission of the Church, the laity, therefore, exercise their apostolate both in the Church and in the world, in both the spiritual and temporal orders. These realms, although distinct, are so connected in the one plan of God that He himself intends in Christ to appropriate the whole universe into a new creation, initially here on earth, fully on the last day. In both orders, the layman, being simultaneously a believer and a citizen, should be constantly led by the same Christian conscience (DAL, N. 5).

2.

Christ, the great prophet, who proclaimed the kingdom of His Father by the testimony of His life and the power of His words, continually fulfills His prophetic office until His final glory is revealed. He does this not only through the hierarchy who teach in His name and with His authority, but also through the laity. For that very purpose He made them His witnesses and gave them understanding of the faith and the grace of speech (cf. Acts 2:17, 18; Rev. 19:10), so that the power of the Gospel might shine forth in their daily social and family life (DCC, N. 35).

3.

For God's Word, through whom all things were made, was himself made flesh and dwelt on the earth of men. Thus He entered the world's history as a perfect man, taking that history up into himself and summarizing it. He himself revealed to us that "God is love" (1 John 4:8). At the same time He taught us that the new command of love was the basic law of human perfection and hence of the world's transformation (CCMW, N. 38).

4.

For the Lord wishes to spread His kingdom by means of the laity also, a kingdom of truth and life, a kingdom of holiness and grace, a kingdom of justice, love, and peace. In this kingdom, creation itself will be delivered out of its slavery to corruption and into the freedom of the glory of the sons of God (cf. Rom. 8:21). Clearly then a great promise and a great mandate are committed to the disciples: "For all are yours, and you are Christ's, and Christ is God's" (1 Cor. 3:23) (DCC, N. 36).

5.

They show themselves to be children of the promise, if, strong in faith and in hope, they make the most of the present time (cf. Eph. 5:16; Col. 4:5), and with patience await the glory that is to come (cf. Rom. 8:25). Let them not, then, hide this hope in the depths of their hearts, but even in the framework of secular life let them express it by a continual turning toward God and by wrestling "against the world rulers of this darkness, against the spiritual forces of wickedness" (Eph. 6:12) (DCC, N. 35).

Citizens of Two Worlds

6.

This Council exhorts Christians, as citizens of two cities, to strive to discharge their earthly duties conscientiously and in response to the Gospel spirit. They are mistaken who, knowing that we do not have here an abiding city, but seek one which is to come, think that they may therefore shirk their earthly responsibilities. For they are forgetting that by the faith itself they are more than ever obliged to measure up to these duties, each according to his own proper vocation (CCMW, N. 43).

7.

God's plan for the world is that men should work together to restore the temporal sphere of things and to develop it unceasingly (DAL, N. 7).

Value of the Temporal Order

8.

It is the task of the whole Church to labor vigorously so that men become capable of constructing the temporal order rightly and directing it to God through Christ. Her pastors must clearly state the principles concerning the purpose of creation and the use of temporal things, and must make available the moral and spiritual aids by which the temporal order can be restored in Christ (DAL, N. 7).

9.

Many elements make up the temporal order: namely, the good things of life and the prosperity of the family, culture, economic affairs, the arts and professions, political institutions, international relations, and other matters of this kind, as well as their development and progress. All of these not only aid in the attainment of man's ultimate goal, but also possess their own intrinsic value. This value has been implanted in them by God, whether they are considered in themselves or as parts of the whole temporal order. "God saw all that he had made, and it was very good" (Gen. 1:31). This natural goodness of theirs takes on a special dignity as a result of their relation to the human person, for whose service they were created. Last of all, it has pleased God to unite all things, both natural and supernatural, in Christ Jesus, "that in all things he may have the first place" (Col. 1:18). This destination, however, not only does not deprive the temporal order of its independence, its proper goals, laws, resources, and significance for human welfare, but rather perfects the temporal order in its own intrinsic strength and excellence and raises it to the level of man's total vocation upon earth (DAL, N. 7).

Laymen Responsible for Renewal of Creation

10.

The laity must take on the renewal of the temporal order as their own special obligation. Led by the light of the Gospel and the mind of the Church, and motivated by Christian love, let them act directly and definitely in the temporal sphere. As citizens they must cooperate with other citizens, using their own particular skills and acting on their own responsibility. Everywhere and in all things they must seek the justice characteristic of God's kingdom. The temporal order must be renewed in such a way that, without the slightest detriment to its own proper laws, it can be brought into conformity with the higher principles of the Christian life and adapted to the shifting circumstances of time, place, and person. Outstanding among the works of this type of apostolate is that of Christian social action. This sacred Synod desires to see it extended now to the whole temporal sphere, including culture (DAL, N. 7).

11.
But the laity, by their very vocation, seek the kingdom of God by engaging in temporal affairs and by ordering them according to the plan of God. They live in the world, that is, in each and in all of the secular professions and occupations. They live in the ordinary circumstances of family and social life, from which the very web of their existence is woven (DCC, N. 31).

12.
They are called there by God so that by exercising their proper functions and being led by the spirit of the Gospel they can work for the sanctification of the world from within, in the manner of leaven. In this way they can make Christ known to others, especially by the testimony of a life resplendent in faith, hope, and charity. The layman is closely involved in temporal affairs of every sort. It is therefore his special task to illumine and organize these affairs in such a way that they may always start out, develop, and persist according to Christ's mind, to the praise of the Creator and the Redeemer (DCC, N. 31).

13.
Because the very plan of salvation requires it, the faithful should learn how to distinguish carefully

between those rights and duties which are theirs as members of the Church, and those which they have as members of human society. Let them strive to harmonize the two, remembering that in every temporal affair they must be guided by a Christian conscience. For even in secular affairs there is no human activity which can be withdrawn from God's dominion. In our own time, however, it is most urgent that this distinction and also this harmony should shine forth as radiantly as possible in the practice of the faithful, so that the mission of the Church may correspond more adequately to the special conditions of the world today. For while it must be recognized that the temporal sphere is governed by its own principles, since it is properly concerned with the interests of this world, that ominous doctrine must be rightly rejected which attempts to build a society with no regard whatever for religion, and which attacks and destroys the religious liberty of its citizens (DCC, N. 36).

14.
With respect to the Christian renewal of the temporal order, laymen should be instructed in the true meaning and value of temporal things, both in themselves and in their relation to the total fulfillment of the human person. They should be trained in the right use of things and the organization of institutions, attentive always to the common good as related to the principles of the moral and social teaching of the Church. Laymen should above all learn the principles and conclusions of this social doctrine so as to become capable of doing their part to advance this doctrine and of rightly applying these principles and conclusions to individual cases (DAL, N. 31).

Secular Life — Laymen's Domain

15.
A secular quality is proper and special to laymen. It is true that those in Holy Orders can at times engage in secular activities, and even have a secular profession. But by reason of their particular vocation they are chiefly and professedly ordained to the sacred ministry. Similarly, by their state in life, religious give splendid and striking testimony that the world cannot be transfigured and offered to God without the spirit of the beatitudes (DCC, N. 31).

16.
Secular duties and activities belong properly although not exclusively to laymen. Therefore acting as citizens of the world, whether individually or socially, they will observe the laws proper to each discipline, and labor to equip themselves with a genuine expertise in their various fields. They will gladly work with men seeking the same goals. Acknowledging the demands of faith and endowed with its force, they will unhesitatingly devise new enterprises, where they are appropriate, and put them into action (CCMW, N. 43).

17.
For when, by the work of his hands or with the aid of technology, man develops the earth so that it can bear fruit and become a dwelling worthy of the whole human family, and when he consciously takes part in the life of social groups, he carries out the design of God. Manifested at the beginning of time, the divine plan is that man should subdue the earth, bring creation to perfection, and develop himself. When a man so acts he simultaneously obeys the great Christian commandment

that he place himself at the service of his brother men (CCMW, N. 57).

18.

Therefore, by their competence in secular fields and by their personal activity, elevated from within by the grace of Christ, let them (the laity) labor vigorously so that by human labor, technical skill, and civic culture created goods may be perfected for the benefit of every last man, according to the design of the Creator and the light of His Word. Let them work to see that created goods are more fittingly distributed among men, and that such goods in their own way lead to general progress in human and Christian liberty. In this manner, through the members of the Church, Christ will progressively illumine the whole of human society with His saving light (DCC, N. 36).

19.

Laymen should also know that it is generally the function of their well-informed Christian conscience to see that the divine law is inscribed in the life of the earthly city. From priests they may look for spiritual light and nourishment. Let the layman not imagine that his pastors are always such experts, that to every problem which arises, however complicated, they can readily give him a concrete solution, or even that such is their mission. Rather, enlightened by Christian wisdom and giving close attention to the teaching authority of the Church, let the layman take on his own distinctive role (CCMW, N. 43).

20.

Therefore, let there be no false opposition between professional and social activities on the one part, and religious life on the other. The Christian who neglects his temporal duties neglects his duties toward his neighbor and even God, and jeopardizes his eternal salvation. Christians should rather rejoice that they can follow the example of Christ, who worked as an artisan. In the exercise of all their earthly activities, they can thereby gather their humane, domestic, professional, social, and technical enterprises into one vital synthesis with religious values, under whose supreme direction all things are harmonized unto God's glory (CCMW, N. 43).

21.

Consequently, even when preoccupied with temporal cares, the laity can and must perform eminently valuable work on behalf of bringing the Gospel to the world. Some of them do all they can to provide sacred services when sacred ministers are lacking or are blocked by a persecuting regime. Many devote themselves entirely to apostolic work. But all ought to cooperate in the spreading and intensifying of the kingdom of God in the world. Therefore, let the laity strive skillfully to acquire a more profound grasp of revealed truth, and insistently beg of God the gift of wisdom (DCC, N. 35).

Social Apostolate Indispensable

22.

The apostolate of the social milieu, that is, the effort to infuse a Christian spirit into the mentality, customs, laws, and structures of the community in which a person lives, is so much the duty and responsibility of the laity that it can never be properly performed by others. In this area the laity can exercise the apostolate of like toward like. It is here that laymen add to the testimony of life the testimony of their speech; it is here in the arena of their labor, profession, studies, residence, leisure, and companionship that laymen have a special opportunity to help their brothers (DAL, N. 13).

23.
Moreover, let the laity also by their combined efforts remedy any institutions and conditions of the world which are customarily an inducement to sin, so that all such things may be conformed to the norms of justice and may favor the practice of virtue rather than hinder it. By so doing, laymen will imbue culture and human activity with moral values. They will better prepare the field of the world for the seed of the Word of God. At the same time they will open wider the Church's doors, through which the message of peace can enter the world (DCC, N. 36).

24.
Christians should recognize that various legitimate though conflicting views can be held concerning the regulation of temporal affairs. They should respect their fellow citizens when they promote such views honorably even by group action. Political parties should foster whatever they judge necessary for the common good. But they should never prefer their own advantage over this same common good (CCMW, N. 75).

25.
The faithful, therefore, must learn the deepest meaning and the value of all creation, and how to

relate it to the praise of God. They must assist one another to live holier lives even in their daily occupations. In this way the world is permeated by the spirit of Christ and more effectively achieves its purpose in justice, charity, and peace. The laity have the principal role in the universal fulfillment of this purpose (DCC, N. 36).

26.
May the faithful, therefore, live in very close union with the men of their time. Let them strive to understand perfectly their way of thinking and feeling, as expressed in their culture. Let them blend modern science and its theories and the understanding of the most recent discoveries with Christian morality and doctrine. Thus their religious practice and morality can keep pace with their scientific knowledge and with an ever-advancing technology. Thus too they will be able to test and interpret all things in a truly Christian spirit (CCMW, N. 62).

Transformation in Christ

27.
Christians, on pilgrimage toward the heavenly city, should seek and savor the things which are above. This duty in no way decreases, but rather increases, the weight of their obligation to work with all men in constructing a more human world. In fact, the mystery of the Christian faith furnishes them with excellent incentives and helps toward discharging this duty more energetically and especially toward uncovering the full meaning of this activity, a meaning which gives human culture its eminent place in the integral vocation of man (CCMW, N. 57).

28.

We do not know the time for the consummation of the earth and of humanity. Nor do we know how all things will be transformed. As deformed by sin, the shape of this world will pass away. But we are taught that God is preparing a new dwelling place and a new earth where justice will abide, and whose blessedness will answer and surpass all the longings for peace which spring up in the human heart (CCMW, N. 39).

29.

Then, with death overcome, the sons of God will be raised up in Christ. What was sown in weakness and corruption will be clothed with incorruptibility. While charity and its fruits endure, all that creation which God made on man's account will be unchained from the bondage of vanity (CCMW, N. 39).

30.

Therefore, while we are warned that it profits a man nothing if he gain the whole world and lose himself, the expectation of a new earth must not weaken but rather stimulate our concern for cultivating this one. For here grows the body of a new human family, a body which even now is able to give some kind of foreshadowing of the new age (CCMW, N. 39).

31.

For after we have obeyed the Lord, and in His Spirit nurtured on earth the values of human dignity, brotherhood, and freedom, and indeed all the good fruits of our nature and enterprise, we will find them again, but freed of stain, burnished and transfigured. This will be so when Christ hands

28.

We do not know the time for the consummation of the earth and of humanity. Nor do we know how all things will be transformed. As deformed by sin, the shape of this world will pass away. But we are taught that God is preparing a new dwelling place and a new earth where justice will abide, and whose blessedness will answer and surpass all the longings for peace which spring up in the human heart (CCMW, N. 39).

29.

Then, with death overcome, the sons of God will be raised up in Christ. What was sown in weakness and corruption will be clothed with incorruptibility. While charity and its fruits endure, all that creation which God made on man's account will be unchained from the bondage of vanity (CCMW, N. 39).

30.

Therefore, while we are warned that it profits a man nothing if he gain the whole world and lose himself, the expectation of a new earth must not weaken but rather stimulate our concern for cultivating this one. For here grows the body of a new human family, a body which even now is able to give some kind of foreshadowing of the new age (CCMW, N. 39).

31.

For after we have obeyed the Lord, and in His Spirit nurtured on earth the values of human dignity, brotherhood, and freedom, and indeed all the good fruits of our nature and enterprise, we will find them again, but freed of stain, burnished and transfigured. This will be so when Christ hands

part, and religious life on the other. The Christian who neglects his temporal duties neglects his duties toward his neighbor and even God, and jeopardizes his eternal salvation. Christians should rather rejoice that they can follow the example of Christ, who worked as an artisan. In the exercise of all their earthly activities, they can thereby gather their humane, domestic, professional, social, and technical enterprises into one vital synthesis with religious values, under whose supreme direction all things are harmonized unto God's glory (CCMW, N. 43).

21.

Consequently, even when preoccupied with temporal cares, the laity can and must perform eminently valuable work on behalf of bringing the Gospel to the world. Some of them do all they can to provide sacred services when sacred ministers are lacking or are blocked by a persecuting regime. Many devote themselves entirely to apostolic work. But all ought to cooperate in the spreading and intensifying of the kingdom of God in the world. Therefore, let the laity strive skillfully to acquire a more profound grasp of revealed truth, and insistently beg of God the gift of wisdom (DCC, N. 35).

Social Apostolate Indispensable

22.

The apostolate of the social milieu, that is, the effort to infuse a Christian spirit into the mentality, customs, laws, and structures of the community in which a person lives, is so much the duty and responsibility of the laity that it can never be properly performed by others. In this area the laity can exercise the apostolate of like toward like. It is here that laymen add to the testimony of life the testimony of their speech; it is here in the arena of their labor, profession, studies, residence, leisure, and companionship that laymen have a special opportunity to help their brothers (DAL, N. 13).

23.

Moreover, let the laity also by their combined efforts remedy any institutions and conditions of the world which are customarily an inducement to sin, so that all such things may be conformed to the norms of justice and may favor the practice of virtue rather than hinder it. By so doing, laymen will imbue culture and human activity with moral values. They will better prepare the field of the world for the seed of the Word of God. At the same time they will open wider the Church's doors, through which the message of peace can enter the world (DCC, N. 36).

24.

Christians should recognize that various legitimate though conflicting views can be held concerning the regulation of temporal affairs. They should respect their fellow citizens when they promote such views honorably even by group action. Political parties should foster whatever they judge necessary for the common good. But they should never prefer their own advantage over this same common good (CCMW, N. 75).

25.

The faithful, therefore, must learn the deepest meaning and the value of all creation, and how to relate it to the praise of God. They must assi another to live holier lives even in their occupations. In this way the world is perm by the spirit of Christ and more effec achieves its purpose in justice, charity, and The laity have the principal role in the un fulfillment of this purpose (DCC, N. 36).

26.

May the faithful, therefore, live in very close with the men of their time. Let them str understand perfectly their way of thinkin feeling, as expressed in their culture. Let blend modern science and its theories an understanding of the most recent discoverie Christian morality and doctrine. Thus religious practice and morality can keep pac their scientific knowledge and with an e vancing technology. Thus too they will be a test and interpret all things in a truly Ch spirit (CCMW, N. 62).

Transformation in Christ

27.

Christians, on pilgrimage toward the heavenl should seek and savor the things which are This duty in no way decreases, but rath creases, the weight of their obligation to with all men in constructing a more human In fact, the mystery of the Christian fait nishes them with excellent incentives and toward discharging this duty more energe and especially toward uncovering the full m of this activity, a meaning which gives l culture its eminent place in the integral vo of man (CCMW, N. 57).

over the kingdom to His Father, a kingdom eternal and universal: "A kingdom of truth and life, of holiness and grace, of justice, love, and peace" (Preface of the Feast of Christ the King). On this earth that kingdom is already present in mystery. When the Lord returns, it will be brought to full flower (CCMW, N. 39).

POINTS TO PONDER

How does Christ wish laymen to assist Him in redeeming creation? (1 through 4)

How do laymen help Christ in this task? (5 through 8)

What is meant by the temporal order? (9 through 14)

Why is a secular quality proper and special to laymen? (15 through 24)

How can laymen permeate the temporal order with the spirit of Christ? (25 through 27)

What is the ultimate goal of the temporal order? (28 through 31)

AUGUST: BUILDERS OF
THE NATIONAL COMMUNITY

SYNOPSIS

Modern conditions demand that the followers of Christ know the people of their nation and join with them in building up their country. As citizens, they should responsibly engage in the public affairs of their nation and promote its common good. One with their countrymen in sincere charity, they should practice effective patriotism, honor the customs of their people, and spread the faith among those with whom they live and have professional connections.

Citizens have the right and duty to participate in the political life of their nation, thereby contributing to its true progress. Laymen should dedicate themselves especially to the protection and full exercise of the human rights of their countrymen. The rights of national minorities must be particularly defended and advanced.

Lawful authority has to ensure that the political community, made up as it is of diverse peoples and groups, is not torn apart. The choice of a particular form of government is left to the free will of its citizens, but every government must conscientiously discharge the burdens of its office, exercise its power within the limits of morality, and work toward the achievement of the common good. Especially must the state provide all its citizens with full opportunities for cultural enrichment and the exercise of human rights.

In an age of increasing socialization laymen must ensure that the true Christian view of man is safeguarded by giving to their countrymen a fully Christian witness. In doing so, they are cooperating with God the Creator, Redeemer and Sanctifier.

DEVELOPMENT

It is the lay vocation to build up the national community (1 through 8).

As citizens they must contribute to the progress of their country (9 through 17).

Those who have political authority must work for the welfare of their people (18 through 22).

Civic and political education are supremely necessary (23 and 24).

Laymen are citizens of two societies (25 through 27).

They must constantly improve the entire social order (28 through 31).

AUGUST
BUILDERS OF
THE NATIONAL COMMUNITY

Build up National Community

1.

Christ himself searched the hearts of men, and led them to divine light through truly human conversation. So also His disciples, profoundly penetrated by the Spirit of Christ, should know the people among whom they live, and should establish contact with them. Thus they themselves can learn by sincere and patient dialogue what treasures a bountiful God has distributed among the nations of the earth. But at the same time, let them try to illumine these treasures with the light of the Gospel, to set them free, and to bring them under the dominion of God their Savior (DCMA, N. 11).

2.

Our own times require of the laity no less zeal. In fact, modern conditions demand that their apostolate be thoroughly broadened and intensified. The constant expansion of population, scientific and technical progress, and the tightening of bonds between men have not only immensely widened the field of the lay apostolate, a field which is for the most part accessible only to them. These developments have themselves raised problems which cry out for the skillful concern and attention of the laity. This apostolate becomes more imperative in view of the fact that many areas of human life have become very largely autonomous. This is as it should be, but it sometimes involves a certain withdrawal from ethical and religious influences, and a certain danger to Christian life. Besides, in many places where priests are very few or, in some instances, are deprived of due freedom in their ministry, the Church could scarcely be present and functioning without the activity of the laity (DAL, N. 1).

3.

To fulfill the mission of the Church in the world, the laity have certain basic needs. They need a life in harmony with their faith, so they can become the light of the world. They need that undeviating honesty which can attract all men to the love of truth and goodness, and finally to the Church and to Christ. They need the kind of fraternal charity which will lead them to share in the living conditions, labors, sorrows, and hope of their brother men, and which will gradually and imperceptibly dispose the hearts of all around them for the saving work of grace. They need a full awareness of their role in building up society, an awareness which will keep them preoccupied with bringing Christian largeheartedness to the fulfillment of their duties, whether family, social, or professional. If laymen can meet all these needs, their behavior will have a penetrating impact, little by little, on the whole circle of their life and labors (DAL, N. 13).

4.

A vast field for the apostolate has been opened up on the national and international levels where most of the laity are called upon to be stewards of Christian wisdom. In loyalty to their country and in faithful fulfillment of their civic obligations, Catholics should feel themselves obliged to promote the true common good. Thus, they should make the weight of their opinion felt, so that civil authority may act with justice, and laws may conform to moral precepts and the common good. Catholics skilled in public affairs and adequately enlightened in faith and Christian doctrine should not refuse to administer public affairs, since by performing this office in a worthy manner they can simultaneously advance the common good and prepare the way for the Gospel (DAL, N. 14).

5.
For the lay faithful fully belong at one and the same time both to the People of God and to civil society. They belong to the nation in which they were born. They have begun to share in its cultural treasures by means of their education. They are joined to its life by manifold social ties. They are cooperating in its progress by their individual efforts, each in his own profession. They feel its problems as their very own, and they are trying to solve them (DCMA, N. 21).

6.
Let them be one with their fellow countrymen in sincere charity, so that there may appear in their way of life a new bond of unity and of universal solidarity, drawn from the mystery of Christ. Let them also spread the faith of Christ among those with whom they live and have professional connections. This obligation is all the more urgent, because very many men can hear of the Gospel and recognize Christ only by means of the laity who are their neighbors. In fact, wherever possible, the laity should be prepared, in more immediate cooperation with the hierarchy, to fulfill a special mission of proclaiming the Gospel and communi-

cating Christian teachings. Thus they can add vigor to the developing Church (DCMA, N. 21).

7.

The Christian faithful, gathered together in the Church out of all nations, "are not marked off from the rest of men by their government, nor by their language, nor by their political institutions" (cf. *Dogmatic Constitution on the Church*, N. 38, footnote 180). So they should live for God and Christ by following the honorable customs of their own nation. As good citizens, they should practice true and effective patriotism. At the same time, let them altogether avoid racial prejudice and bitter nationalism, fostering instead a universal love for man. In the attainment of these goals, laymen have the greatest importance and deserve special attention. These are those Christians who have been incorporated into Christ by Baptism and who live in the world. For it is up to them, imbued with the spirit of Christ, to be a leaven animating temporal affairs from within, disposing them always to become as Christ would wish them (DCMA, N. 15).

8.

But it is not enough for the Christian people to be present and organized in a given nation. Nor is it enough for them to carry out an apostolate of good example. They are organized and present for the purpose of announcing Christ to their non-Christian fellow citizens by word and deed, and of aiding them toward the full reception of Christ (DCMA, N. 15).

Must Contribute to Progress

9.

Citizens, for their part, should remember that they have the right and duty, which must be recognized by civil authority, to contribute according to their ability to the true progress of their own community. Especially in underdeveloped areas, where all resources must be put to urgent use, those men gravely endanger the public good who allow their resources to remain unproductive or who deprive their community of the material and spiritual aids it needs. The personal right of migration, however, is not to be impugned (CCMW, N. 65).

10.
Citizens should develop a generous and loyal devotion to their country, but without any narrowing of mind. In other words, they must always look simultaneously to the welfare of the whole human family, which is tied together by the manifold bonds linking races, peoples, and nations (CCMW, N. 75).

11.
Let Christians appreciate their special and personal vocation in the political community. This vocation requires that they give conspicuous example of devotion to the sense of duty and of service to the advancement of the common good. Thus they can also show in practice how authority is to be harmonized with freedom, personal initiative with consideration for the bonds uniting the whole social body, and necessary unity with beneficial diversity (CCMW, N. 75).

12.
Our times have witnessed profound changes too in the institutions of peoples and in the ways that peoples are joined together. These changes are resulting from the cultural, economic, and social

evolution of these same peoples. The changes are having a great impact on the life of the political community, especially with regard to universal rights and duties both in the exercise of civil liberty and in the attainment of the common good, and with regard to the regulation of the relations of citizens among themselves, and with public authority (CCMW, N. 73).

13.
From a keener awareness of human dignity there arises in many parts of the world a desire to establish a political-juridical order in which personal rights can gain better protection. These include the rights of free assembly, of common action, of expressing personal opinions, and of professing a religion both privately and publicly. For the protection of personal rights is a necessary condition for the active participation of citizens, whether as individuals or collectively, in the life and government of the state (CCMW, N. 73).

14.
Among numerous people, cultural, economic, and social progress has been accompanied by the desire to assume a larger role in organizing the life of the political community. In many consciences there is a growing intent that the rights of national minorities be honored while at the same time these minorities honor their duties toward the political community. In addition men are learning more every day to respect the opinions and religious beliefs of others. At the same time a broader spirit of cooperation is taking hold. Thus all citizens, and not just a privileged few, are actually able to enjoy personal rights (CCMW, N. 73).

15.

No better way exists for attaining a truly human political life than by fostering an inner sense of justice, benevolence, and service for the common good, and by strengthening basic beliefs about the true nature of the political, and about the proper exercise and limits of public authority (CCMW, N. 73).

16.

If every citizen is to feel inclined to take part in the activities of the various groups which make up the social body, these must offer advantages which will attract members and dispose them to serve others. We can justly consider that the future of humanity lies in the hands of those who are strong enough to provide coming generations with reasons for living and hoping (CCMW, N. 31).

17.

Many different people go to make up the political community, and these can lawfully incline toward diverse ways of doing things. Now, if the political community is not to be torn to pieces as each man follows his own viewpoint, authority is needed. This authority must dispose the energies of the whole citizenry toward the common good, not mechanically or despotically, but primarily as a moral force which depends on freedom and the conscientious discharge of the burdens of any office which has been undertaken. It is therefore obvious that the political community and public authority are based on human nature and hence belong to an order of things divinely foreordained. At the same time the choice of government and the method of selecting leaders is left to the free will of citizens (CCMW, N. 74).

Welfare of People:
Responsibility of Political Authority

18.

It also follows that political authority, whether in the community as such or in institutions representing the state, must always be exercised within the limits of morality and on behalf of the dynamically conceived common good, according to a juridical order enjoying legal status. When such is the case citizens are conscience bound to obey. This fact clearly reveals the responsibility, dignity, and importance of those who govern. Hence the political community exists for that common good in which the community finds its full justification and meaning, and from which it derives its pristine and proper right. Now, the common good embraces the sum of those conditions of social life by which individuals, families, and groups can achieve their own fulfillment in a relatively thorough and ready way (CCMW, N. 74).

19.

The common welfare of society consists in the entirety of those conditions of social life under which men enjoy the possibility of achieving their own perfection in a certain fullness of measure and also with some relative ease. Hence this welfare consists chiefly in the protection of the rights, and in the performance of the duties, of the human person. Therefore, the care of the right to religious freedom devolves upon the people as a whole, upon social groups, upon government, and upon the Church and other religious communities, in virtue of the duty of all toward the common welfare, and in the manner proper to each. The protection and promotion of the inviolable rights of man ranks among the essential duties of government (DRF, N. 6).

20.
It is in full accord with human nature that juridical-political structures should, with ever better success and without any discrimination, afford all their citizens the chance to participate freely and actively in establishing the constitutional bases of a political community, governing the state, determining the scope and purpose of various institutions, and choosing leaders. Hence let all citizens be mindful of their simultaneous right and duty to vote freely in the interest of advancing the common good. The Church regards as worthy of praise and consideration the work of those who, as a service to others, dedicate themselves to the welfare of the state and undertake the burdens of this task (CCMW, N. 75).

21.
Authorities must beware of hindering family, social, or cultural groups, as well as intermediate bodies and institutions. They must not deprive them of their lawful and effective activity, but should rather strive to promote them willingly and in an orderly fashion. For their part, citizens both as individuals and in association should be on guard against granting government too much authority and inappropriately seeking from it excessive conveniences and advantages, with a consequent weakening of the sense of responsibility on the part of individuals, families, and social groups (CCMW, N. 75).

22.
Individuals, families, and various groups which compose the civic community are aware of their

own insufficiency in the matter of establishing a fully human condition of life. They see the need for that wider community in which each would daily contribute his energies toward the ever better attainment of the common good. It is for this reason that they set up the political community in its manifold expressions (CCMW, N. 74).

Necessity of Civic and Political Education

23.

Civic and political education is today supremely necessary for the people, especially young people. Such education should be painstakingly provided, so that all citizens can make their contribution to the political community. Let those who are suited for it, or can become so, prepare themselves for the difficult but most honorable art of politics. Let them work to exercise this art without thought of personal convenience and without benefit of bribery. Prudently and honorably let them fight against injustice and oppression, the arbitrary rule of one man or one party, and lack of tolerance. Let them devote themselves to the welfare of all sincerely and fairly, indeed with charity and political courage (CCMW, N. 75).

24.

For the rest, it is incumbent upon the state to provide all citizens with the opportunity to acquire an appropriate degree of cultural enrichment, and with the proper preparation for exercising their civic duties and rights. Therefore, the state itself ought to protect the right of children to receive an adequate schooling. It should be vigilant about the ability of teachers and the excellence of their training. It should look after the health of students and, in general, promote the whole school enterprise. But it must keep in mind the principle of subsidiarity, so that no kind of school monopoly arises. For such a monopoly would militate against the native rights of the human person, the development and spread of culture itself, the peaceful association of citizens, and the pluralism which exists today in very many societies (DCE, N. 6).

Citizens of Two Societies

25.
It is highly important, especially in pluralistic societies, that a proper view exist of the relation between the political community and the Church. Thus the faithful will be able to make a clear distinction between what a Christian conscience leads them to do in their own name as citizens, whether as individuals or in association, and what they do in the name of the Church and in union with her shepherds (CCMW, N. 76).

26.
Often enough the Christian view of things will itself suggest some specific solution in certain circumstances. Yet it happens rather frequently, and legitimately so, that with equal sincerity some of the faithful will disagree with others on a given matter. Even against the intentions of their proponents, however, solutions proposed on one side or the other may be easily confused by many people with the Gospel message. Hence it is necessary for people to remember that no one is allowed in the aforementioned situations to appropriate the Church's authority for his opinion. They should always try to enlighten one another through honest discussion, preserving mutual

charity and caring above all for the common good (CCMW, N. 43).

27.
Man's social nature makes it evident that the progress of the human person and the advance of society itself hinge on each other. For the beginning, the subject and the goal of all social institutions is and must be the human person, which for its part and by its very nature stands completely in need of social life. This social life is not something added on to man. Hence, through his dealings with others, through reciprocal duties, and through fraternal dialogue he develops all his gifts and is able to rise to his destiny (CCMW, N. 25).

Improvement of the Social Order

28.
Among those social ties which man needs for his development some, like the family and political community, relate with greater immediacy to his innermost nature. In our era, for various reasons, reciprocal ties and mutual dependencies increase day by day and give rise to a variety of associations and organizations, both public and private. This development, which is called socialization, while certainly not without its dangers, brings with it many advantages with respect to consolidating and increasing the qualities of the human person, and safeguarding his rights (CCMW, N. 25).

29.
This social order requires constant improvement. It must be founded on truth, built on justice, and animated by love; in freedom it should grow every day toward a more humane balance. An improvement in attitudes and widespread changes in

society will have to take place if these objectives are to be gained (CCMW, N. 26).

30.
Closely united with men in their life and work, Christ's disciples hope to render to others true witness of Christ, and to work for their salvation, even when they are not able to proclaim Christ fully. For they are not seeking a mere material progress and prosperity for men, but are promoting their dignity and brotherly union, teaching those religious and moral truths which Christ illumined with His light. In this way, they are gradually opening up a wider approach to God. Thus too they help men to attain to salvation by love for God and neighbor. And the mystery of Christ begins to shine forth. In this mystery the new man has appeared, created according to God (cf. Eph. 4:24). In it the love of God is revealed (DCMA, N. 12).

31.
Furthermore, in collaborating as citizens of this world in whatever pertains to the upbuilding and operation of the temporal order, the laity should, under the light of faith, seek for loftier motives of action in their family, professional, cultural, and social life, and make them known to others when the occasion arises. Let them be aware that by so doing they are cooperating with God the creator, redeemer, and sanctifier and are giving praise to Him (DAL, N. 16).

POINTS TO PONDER

Why do modern conditions demand an intensified lay apostolate? (1 through 3)

Why must laymen be good citizens? (4 through 8)

What is required of laymen as citizens? (9 through 11)

What changes are occurring in political communities today? (12 through 16)

What are the responsibilities of those holding political authority? (17 through 21)

How can the nation assist its citizens in our time? (22 through 24)

What relationship exists between the nation and the Church? (25 through 27)

Is socialization acceptable today? (28 and 29)

How can laymen be a leaven among their countrymen? (30 and 31)

SEPTEMBER: BUILDERS OF THE
INTERNATIONAL COMMUNITY

SYNOPSIS

It is God's will that all men constitute one family and treat one another as brothers. Since each human person bears the image of his maker, love of neighbor is, with love of God, the first and greatest commandment.

Renewal can only occur when laymen individually and through organizations extend their range of charities to the very ends of the earth, touching every person and caring for every need. The global nature of the Church's mission also necessitates apostolic enterprises on the international level. A primary function of the lay apostolate is to promote solidarity and brotherhood among all peoples. God intended the goods of the earth to be shared by all men of all nations and laymen must be committed to seeing that this is achieved.

Christians should ensure that relations among peoples are genuine fraternal exchanges in which each party is both a giver and a receiver. They should establish associations which will guarantee among nations a just distribution of the resources of the earth and scientific technology, particularly in underdeveloped countries.

Human interdependence expands from day to day. With it should be promoted a true communion between persons. One outgrowth of this can be a lasting peace; another, the recognition that we are all brothers under God. The human family is becoming a single world community. The community of Christ's followers should collaborate with other men of good will in creating an international order based upon freedom and brotherhood. The pilgrim Church is intimately linked with this world community.

DEVELOPMENT

God has willed that all men form one human family (1 and 2).

Brotherhood in this family is based upon love (3 through 5).

Love must be demonstrated by positive social action (6 through 13).

Christians must support cooperation within the international community (14 through 17).

Underdeveloped nations need special assistance (18 and 19).

Interdependence among peoples becomes daily more real (20 through 27).

Christ's followers must work for the renovation of the world (28 through 30).

SEPTEMBER

BUILDERS OF THE
INTERNATIONAL COMMUNITY

God Wills One Human Family

1.

God, who has fatherly concern for everyone, has willed that all men should constitute one family and treat one another in a spirit of brotherhood. For having been created in the image of God, who "from one man has created the whole human race and made them live all over the face of the earth" (Acts 17:26), all men are called to one and the same goal, namely, God himself. Indeed, the Lord Jesus, when He prayed to the Father, "that all may be one ... as we are one" (John 17:21, 22) opened up vistas closed to human reason. For He implied a certain likeness between the union of the divine Persons, and in the union of God's sons in truth and charity. This likeness reveals that man, who is the only creature on earth which God willed for itself, cannot fully find himself except through a sincere gift of himself (CCMW, N. 24).

2.

To those, therefore, who believe in divine love, He gives assurance that the way of love lies open to all men and that the effort to establish a universal brotherhood is not a hopeless one. He cautions them at the same time that this love is not something to be reserved for important matters, but must be pursued chiefly in the ordinary circumstances of life (CCMW, N. 38).

Brotherhood Based on Love

3.

For this reason, love for God and neighbor is the first and greatest commandment. Sacred Scripture, however, teaches us that the love of God cannot be separated from love of neighbor: "If there is any other commandment, it is summed up in this saying, thou shalt love thy neighbor as thyself . . . Love therefore is the fulfillment of the Law" (Rom. 13:9, 10; cf. 1 John 4:20). To men growing daily more dependent on one another, and to a world becoming more unified every day, this truth proves to be of paramount importance (CCMW, N. 24).

4.

That the exercise of such charity may rise above any deficiencies in fact and even in appearance, certain fundamentals must be observed. Thus attention is to be paid to the image of God in which our neighbor has been created, and also to Christ the Lord to whom is really offered whatever is given to a needy person. The freedom and dignity of the person being helped should be respected with the utmost delicacy, and the purity of one's charitable intentions should not be stained by a quest for personal advantage or by any thirst for domination. The demands for justice should first be satisfied, lest the giving of what is due in justice be represented as the offering of a charitable gift. Not only the effects but also the causes of various ills must be removed. Help should be given in such a way that the recipients may gradually be freed from dependence on others and become self-sufficient (DAL, N. 8).

5.

The grace of renewal cannot flourish in communities unless each of them extends its range of charities to the ends of the earth, and devotes to those far off a concern similar to that which it bestows on those who are its own members. Thus the whole community prays, collaborates, and exercises activity among the nations through those of its sons whom God chooses for this most excellent task (DCMA, N. 37).

Love through Positive Social Action

6.

At the present time, when the means of communication have grown more rapid, the distances between men have been overcome in a sense, and the inhabitants of the whole world have become like members of a single family, these actions and works have grown much more urgent and extensive. These charitable enterprises can and should reach out to absolutely every person and every need. Wherever there are people in need of food and drink, clothing, housing, medicine, employment, education; wherever men lack the facilities necessary for living a truly human life or are tormented by hardships or poor health, or suffer exile or imprisonment, there Christian charity should seek them out and find them, console them with eager care and relieve them with the gift of help. This obligation is imposed above all upon every prosperous person and nation (DAL, N. 8).

7.

Now, in view of the progress of social institutions and the fast-moving pace of modern society, the global nature of the Church's mission requires that apostolic enterprises of Catholics should increasingly develop organized forms at the international level. Catholic international organizations will more effectively achieve their purpose if the groups comprising them, as well as their members, are involved more closely and individually in these international organizations (DAL, N. 19).

8.

Among the signs of our times, the irresistibly increasing sense of solidarity among all peoples is especially noteworthy. It is a function of the lay apostolate to promote this awareness zealously and to transform it into a sincere and genuine sense of brotherhood. Furthermore, the laity should be informed about the international field and about the questions and solutions, theoretical as well as practical, which arise in this field, especially with respect to developing nations (DAL, N. 14).

9.

God intended the earth and all that it contains for the use of every human being and people. Thus, as all men follow justice and unite in charity, created goods should abound for them on a reasonable basis. Whatever the forms of ownership may be, as adapted to the legitimate institutions of people according to diverse and changeable circumstances, attention must always be paid to the universal purpose for which created goods were meant. In using them, therefore, a man should regard his lawful possessions not merely as his own but also as common property in the sense that they should accrue to the benefit of not only himself but of others (CCMW, N. 69).

10.

Today the bonds of mutual dependence become increasingly close between all citizens and all the peoples of the world. The universal common good needs to be intelligently pursued and more effectively achieved. Hence it is now necessary for the family of nations to create for themselves an order that corresponds to modern obligations, particularly with reference to those numerous regions still laboring under intolerable need (CCMW, N. 84).

11.

Christians, especially young people, are to be praised and supported, therefore, when they volunteer their services to help other men and nations. Indeed, it is the duty of the whole People of God, following the word and example of the bishops, to do their utmost to alleviate the sufferings of the modern age. As was the custom anciently in the Church, they should meet this obligation out of the substance of their goods, and not only out of what is superfluous. Without being inflexible and completely uniform, the collection and distribution of aid should be conducted in an orderly fashion in dioceses, nations, and throughout the entire world. (Wherever it seems appropriate, this activity of Catholics should be carried on in unison with other Christian brothers.) For the spirit of charity does not forbid but rather requires that charitable activity be exercised in a provident and orderly manner. Therefore, it is essential for those who intend to dedicate themselves to the service of the developing nations to be properly trained in suitable institutions (CCMW, N. 88).

12.

Furthermore, let the faithful take part in the strivings of those peoples who are waging war on famine, ignorance, and disease and thereby struggling to better their way of life and to secure peace in the world. In this activity, the faithful should be eager to offer their prudent aid to projects sponsored by public and private organizations, by governments, by international agencies, by various Christian communities, and even by non-Christian religions (DCMA, N. 12).

13.
All who work in or give help to foreign nations must remember that relations among peoples should be a genuine fraternal exchange in which each party is at the same time a giver and a receiver. Whether their purpose is international affairs, private business, or leisure, traveling Christians should remember that they are journeying heralds of Christ wherever they go, and should act accordingly (DAL, N. 14).

Support Cooperation within Community

14.
An outstanding form of international activity on the part of Christians undoubtedly consists in the cooperative efforts which, as individuals and in groups, they make to institutes established for the encouragement of cooperation among nations. The same is true of their efforts to establish such agencies. There are also various international Catholic associations which can serve in many ways to construct a peaceful and fraternal community of nations. These deserve to be strengthened by an increase in the number of well-qualified associates and in the needed resources. Let them be fortified too by a suitable coordination of their energies. For today effective action as well as the need for dialogue demand joint projects. Moreover, such associations contribute much to the development of a universal outlook — something certainly appropriate for Catholics. They also help

to form an awareness of genuine universal solidarity and responsibility (CCMW, N. 90).

15.
This goal will come about more effectively if the faithful themselves, conscious of their responsibility as men and as Christians, strive to stir up in their own area of influence a willingness to cooperate readily with the international community. In both religious and civic education, special care must be given to the proper formation of youth in this respect (CCMW, N. 89).

16.
Therefore, all sons of the Church should have a lively awareness of their responsibility to the world. They should foster in themselves a truly catholic spirit. They should spend their energies in the work of evangelization (DCMA, N. 36).

17.
They should constantly foster a feeling for their own diocese, of which the parish is a kind of cell, and be ever ready at their bishop's invitation to participate in diocesan projects. Indeed, if the needs of cities and rural areas are to be met, laymen should not limit their cooperation to the parochial or diocesan boundaries but strive to extend it to interparochial, interdiocesan, national, and international fields, the more so because the daily increase in population mobility, the growth of mutual bonds, and the ease of communication no longer allow any sector of society to remain closed in upon itself. Thus they should be concerned about the needs of the People of God dispersed throughout the world. They should above all make missionary activity their own by

giving material or even personal assistance. For it is a duty and honor for Christians to return to God a part of the good things they receive from Him (DAL, N. 10).

Underdeveloped Nations Need Special Assistance

18.
Finally, laymen should willingly offer socioeconomic cooperation to peoples undergoing development. This cooperation is all the more praiseworthy to the extent that it concerns itself with founding institutions which touch on the basic structures of social life, or which are oriented to the training of those who bear the responsibility for government (DCMA, N. 41).

19.
Therefore, the laity should hold in high esteem and, according to their ability, aid the works of charity and projects for social assistance, whether public or private, including international programs whereby effective help is given to needy individuals and peoples. In so doing, they should cooperate with all men of good will (DAL, N. 8).

Interdependence among Peoples

20.
Every day human interdependence grows more tightly drawn and spreads by degrees over the whole world. As a result the common good, that is, the sum of those conditions of social life which allow social groups and their individual members relatively thorough and ready access to their own fulfillment, today takes on an increasingly universal complexion and consequently involves rights and duties with respect to the whole human race. Every social group must take account of the needs

and legitimate aspirations of other groups, and even of the general welfare of the entire human family (CCMW, N. 26).

21.
One of the salient features of the modern world is the growing interdependence of men one on the other, a development very largely promoted by modern technical advances. Nevertheless, brotherly dialogue among men does not reach its perfection on the level of technical progress, but on the deeper level of interpersonal relationships. These demand a mutual respect for the full spiritual dignity of the person. Christian revelation contributes greatly to the promotion of this communion between persons, and at the same time leads us to a deeper understanding of the laws of social life which the Creator has written into man's spiritual and moral nature (CCMW, N. 23).

22.
That earthly peace which arises from love of neighbor symbolizes and results from the peace of Christ who comes forth from God the Father. For by His cross the incarnate Son, the Prince of Peace, reconciled all men with God. By thus restoring the unity of all men in one people and one body, He slew hatred in His own flesh. After being lifted up on high by His Resurrection, He poured the Spirit of love into the hearts of men. For this reason, all Christians are urgently summoned "to practice the truth in love" (Eph. 4:15) and to join with all true peacemakers in pleading for peace and bringing it about (CCMW, N. 78).

23.
It is our clear duty, then, to strain every muscle as we work for the time when all war can be com-

pletely outlawed by international consent. This goal undoubtedly requires the establishment of some universal public authority acknowledged as such by all, and endowed with effective power to safeguard, on the behalf of all, security, regard for justice, and respect for rights (CCMW, N. 82).

24.

We cannot in truthfulness call upon that God who is the Father of all if we refuse to act in a brotherly way toward certain men, created though they be to God's image. A man's relationship with God the Father and his relationship with his brother men are so linked together that Scripture says: "He who does not love does not know God" (1 John 4:8). The ground is therefore removed from every theory or practice which leads to a distinction between men or peoples in the matter of human dignity and the rights which flow from it (DRCN-CR, N. 5).

25.

Christians should collaborate willingly and wholeheartedly in establishing an international order involving genuine respect for all freedoms and amicable brotherhood between all men. This objective is all the more pressing since the greater part of the world is still suffering from so much poverty that it is as if Christ himself were crying out in these poor to beg the charity of the disciples (CCMW, N. 88).

26.

In view of the immense hardships which still afflict the majority of men today, the Council regards it as most opportune that some agency of the universal Church be set up for the world-wide promotion of justice for the poor and of Christ's kind love for them. The role of such an organization will be to stimulate the Catholic community to foster progress in needy regions, and social justice on the international scene (CCMW, N. 90).

27.
Finally, this Council desires that by way of fulfilling their role properly in the international community, Catholics should seek to cooperate actively and in a positive manner both with their separated brothers, who together with them profess the Gospel of love, and with all men thirsting for true peace (CCMW, N. 90).

Work Toward Renovation of the World
28.
Through his labors and his native endowments man has ceaselessly striven to better his life. Today, however, especially with the help of science and technology, he has extended his mastery over nearly the whole of nature and continues to do so. Thanks primarily to increased opportunities for many kinds of interchange among nations, the human family is gradually recognizing that it comprises a single world community and is making itself so. Hence many benefits once looked for, especially from heavenly powers, man has now enterprisingly procured for himself (CCMW, N. 33).

29.
The joys and the hopes, the griefs and the anxieties of the men of this age, especially those who are poor or in any way afflicted, these too are the joys and hopes, the griefs and anxieties of the followers of Christ. Indeed, nothing genuinely

human fails to raise an echo in their hearts. For theirs is a community composed of men. United in Christ, they are led by the Holy Spirit in their journey to the kingdom of their Father and they have welcomed the news of salvation which is meant for every man. This is why this community realizes that it is truly and intimately linked with mankind and its history (CCMW, N. 1).

30.
Therefore, the promised restoration which we are awaiting has already begun in Christ, is carried forward in the mission of the Holy Spirit, and through Him continues in the Church. There we learn through faith the meaning, too, of our temporal life, as we perform, with hope of good things to come, the task committed to us in this world by the Father, and work out our salvation (cf. Phil. 2:12).

The final age of the world has already come upon us (cf. 1 Cor. 10:11). The renovation of the world has been irrevocably decreed and in this age is already anticipated in some real way. For even now on this earth the Church is marked with a genuine though imperfect holiness. However, until there is a new heaven and a new earth where justice dwells (cf. 2 Peter 3:13), the pilgrim Church in her sacraments and institutions, which pertain to this present time, takes on the appearance of this passing world. She herself dwells among creatures who groan and travail in pain until now and await the revelation of the sons of God (cf. Rom. 8:19-22) (DCC, N. 48).

POINTS TO PONDER

Has God really willed a universal brotherhood among men? (1 and 2)

How can this brotherhood be achieved? (3 through 5)

Why are present conditions conducive for solidarity among all peoples? (6 through 8)

What responsibilities do people have toward the common good? (9 through 13)

How can laymen use international associations to promote brotherhood? (14 through 19)

Why must brotherhood be a real communion among persons? (20 through 27)

Why is the pilgrim Church intimately linked with mankind and its history? (28 through 30)

OCTOBER: MARRIED LIFE

SYNOPSIS

The apostolate of married people is of unique importance in the Church and the world. God established the intimate partnership of married life and endowed it with benefits for the couple and their children, as well as for society. Christ so blessed married love that the partners are sacramentally consecrated to the duties of their vocation: the couple are witnesses to each other of their mutual faith in and love for Christ. Their mutual love involves their whole person and leads them to a free gift of themselves, expressed in the marriage act. Hallowed by faithfulness, this love remains intact in all the circumstances of life. All of this provides excellent training for the lay apostolate.

Marriage and conjugal love are ordained to the begetting of children, the supreme gift of married life. In having children the couple cooperate with their Creator and Savior to enrich the family of man. Certain modern conditions make it difficult for many couples to live harmonious lives and beget children, but in questions regarding the transmission of life, morality must be determined by objective standards since this always has a bearing on the couple's eternal destiny.

Spouses should work together for their mutual sanctification, seeking holiness through faithful love and mutual encouragement, because they are co-sharers in grace. It is the supreme task of their apostolate to uphold the sacred and unbreakable character of the marriage bond. In so doing, they reflect and partake in the unity and fruitful love which exists between Christ and His Church.

DEVELOPMENT

Marriage has been established by God (1 through 5).

Love is the foundation of marriage (6 through 15).

The couple must constantly deepen that love (16 through 18).

Children are the fruit of chaste married love (19 through 21).

The transmission of life is a sacred responsibility (22 through 26).

Married people have their own path to holiness (27 through 31).

OCTOBER
MARRIED LIFE

Marriage Was Established by God

1.

In the Church, there is diversity of service but unity of purpose. Christ conferred on the apostles and their successors the duty of teaching, sanctifying, and ruling in His name and power. But the laity, too, share in the priestly, prophetic, and royal office of Christ and therefore have their own role to play in the mission of the whole People of God in the Church and in the world (DAL, N. 2).

2.

But God did not create man as a solitary. For from the beginning "male and female he created them" (Gen. 1:27). Their companionship produces the primary form of interpersonal communion. For by his innermost nature man is a social being, and unless he relates himself to others he can neither live nor develop his potential (CCMW, N. 12).

3.

Since the Creator of all things has established the conjugal partnership as the beginning and basis of human society and, by His grace, has made it a great mystery in Christ and the Church (cf. Eph. 5:32), the apostolate of married persons and of families is of unique importance for the Church and civil society (DAL, N. 11).

4.

The intimate partnership of married life and love has been established by the Creator and qualified by His laws. It is rooted in the conjugal covenant of irrevocable personal consent. Hence, by that human act whereby spouses mutually bestow and accept each other, a relationship arises which by divine will and in the eyes of society too is a lasting one. For the good of the spouses and their offspring as well as of society, the existence of this sacred bond no longer depends on human decision alone (CCMW, N. 48).

The Foundation of Marriage Is Love

5.
For God himself is the author of Matrimony, endowed as it is with various benefits and purposes. All of these have a very decisive bearing on the continuation of the human race, on the personal development and eternal destiny of the individual members of a family, and on the destiny, stability, peace, and prosperity of the family itself and of human society as a whole. By their very nature, the institution of Matrimony itself and conjugal love are ordained for the procreation and education of children, and find in them their ultimate crown (CCMW, N. 48).

6.
Thus a man and a woman, who by the marriage covenant of conjugal love "are no longer two, but one flesh" (Matt. 19:6), render mutual help and service to each other through an intimate union of their persons and of their actions. Through this union they experience the meaning of their oneness and attain to it with growing perfection day by day. As a mutual gift of two persons, this intimate union, as well as the good of the children, imposes total fidelity on the spouses and argues for an unbreakable oneness between them (CCMW, N. 48).

7.

Christ the Lord abundantly blessed this many-faceted love, welling up as it does from the fountain of divine love and structured as it is on the model of His union with the Church. For as God of old made himself present to His people through a covenant of love and fidelity, so now the Savior of men and the Spouse of the Church comes into the lives of married Christians through the sacrament of Matrimony. He abides with them thereafter so that, just as He loved the Church and handed himself over on her behalf, the spouses may love each other with perpetual fidelity through mutual self-bestowal (CCMW, N. 48).

8.

Authentic married love is caught up into divine love and is governed and enriched by Christ's redeeming power and the saving activity of the Church. Thus this love can lead the spouses to God with powerful effect and can aid and strengthen them in the sublime office of being a father or a mother (CCMW, N. 48).

9.

For this reason, Christian spouses have a special sacrament by which they are fortified and receive a kind of consecration in the duties and dignity of their state. By virtue of this sacrament, as spouses fulfill their conjugal and family obligations, they are penetrated with the spirit of Christ. This spirit suffuses their whole lives with faith, hope, and charity. Thus they increasingly advance their own perfection, as well as their mutual sanctification, and hence contribute jointly to the glory of God (CCMW, N. 48).

10.

In connection with this function, that state of life which is sanctified by a special sacrament is obviously of great value, namely, married and family life. For where Christianity pervades a whole way of life and ever increasingly transforms it, there will exist both the practice and an excellent school of the lay apostolate. In such a home, husband and wife find their proper vocation in being witnesses to one another and to their children of faith in Christ and love for Him. The Christian family loudly proclaims both the present virtues of the kingdom of God and the hope of a blessed life to come (DCC, N. 35).

11.

The Biblical Word of God several times urges the betrothed and the married to nourish and develop their wedlock by pure conjugal love and undivided affection. Many men of our own age also highly regard true love between husband and wife as it manifests itself in a variety of ways depending on the worthy customs of various peoples and times (CCMW, N. 49).

12.

This love is an eminently human one since it is directed from one person to another through an affection of the will. It involves the good of the whole person. Therefore it can enrich the expressions of body and mind with a unique dignity, ennobling these expressions as special ingredients and signs of the friendship distinctive of marriage. This love the Lord has judged worthy of special gifts, healing, perfecting, and exalting gifts of grace and of charity (CCMW, N. 49).

13.
Such love, merging the human with the divine, leads the spouses to a free and mutual gift of themselves, a gift proving itself by gentle affection and by deed. Such love pervades the whole of their lives. Indeed, by its generous activity it grows better and grows greater. Therefore it far excels mere erotic inclination, which, selfishly pursued, soon enough fades wretchedly away (CCMW, N. 49).

14.
This love is uniquely expressed and perfected through the marital act. The actions within marriage by which the couple are united intimately and chastely are noble and worthy ones. Expressed in a manner which is truly human, these actions signify and promote that mutual self-giving by which the spouses enrich each other with a joyful and thankful will (CCMW, N. 49).

15.
Sealed by mutual faithfulness and hallowed above all by Christ's sacrament, this love remains steadfastly true in body and in mind, in bright days or dark. It will never be profaned by adultery or divorce. Firmly established by the Lord, the unity of marriage will radiate from the equal personal dignity of wife and husband, a dignity acknowledged by mutual and total love (CCMW, N. 49).

Couple Should Constantly Deepen Love

16.
The steady fulfillment of the duties of this Christian vocation demands notable virtue. For this reason, strengthened by grace for holiness of life,

the couple will painstakingly cultivate and pray for constancy of love, large-heartedness, and the spirit of sacrifice (CCMW, N. 49).

17.
Authentic conjugal love will be more highly prized, and wholesome public opinion created regarding it, if Christian couples give outstanding witness to faithfulness and harmony in that same love, and to their concern for educating their children; also, if they do their part in bringing about the needed cultural, psychological, and social renewal on behalf of marriage and the family (CCMW, N. 49).

18.
Especially in the heart of their own families, young people should be aptly and seasonably instructed about the dignity, duty, and expression of married love. Trained thus in the cultivation of chastity, they will be able at a suitable age to enter a marriage of their own after an honorable courtship (CCMW, N. 49).

Children Are Fruit of Married Love

19.
Marriage and conjugal love are by their nature ordained toward the begetting and educating of children. Children are really the supreme gift of marriage and contribute very substantially to the welfare of their parents. The God himself who said, "It is not good for man to be alone" (Gen. 2:18) and "who made man from the beginning male and female" (Matt. 19:4), wishes to share with man a certain special participation in His own creative work. Thus He blessed male and female, saying: "Increase and multiply" (Gen. 1:28) (CCMW, N. 50).

20.

Hence, while not making the other purposes of Matrimony of less account, the true practice of conjugal love, and the whole meaning of the family life which results from it, have this aim: that the couple be ready with stout hearts to cooperate with the love of the creator and the savior, who through them will enlarge and enrich His own family day by day (CCMW, N. 50).

21.

Marriage to be sure is not instituted solely for procreation. Rather, its very nature as an unbreakable compact between persons, and the welfare of the children, both demand that the mutual love of the spouses, too, be embodied in a rightly ordered manner, that it grow and ripen. Therefore, marriage persists as a whole manner and communion of life, and maintains its value and indissolubility, even when offspring are lacking — despite, rather often, the very intense desire of the couple (CCMW, N. 50).

Transmission of Life — A Sacred Responsibility

22.

This Council realizes that certain modern conditions often keep couples from arranging their married lives harmoniously, and that they find themselves in circumstances where at least temporarily the size of their families should not be increased. As a result, the faithful exercise of love and the full intimacy of their lives are hard to maintain. But where the intimacy of married life is broken off, it is not rare for its faithfulness to be imperiled and its quality of fruitfulness ruined. For then the upbringing of the children and the courage to accept new ones are both endangered (CCMW, N. 51).

23.
To these problems there are those who presume to offer dishonorable solutions. Indeed, they do not recoil from the taking of life. But the Church issues a reminder that a true contradiction cannot exist between the divine laws pertaining to the transmission of life and those pertaining to the fostering of authentic conjugal love (CCMW, N. 51).

24.
For God, the Lord of life, has conferred on men the surpassing ministry of safeguarding life — a ministry which must be fulfilled in a manner which is worthy of man. Therefore from the moment of its conception life must be guarded with the greatest care, while abortion and infanticide are unspeakable crimes. The sexual characteristics of man and the human faculty of reproduction wonderfully exceed the dispositions of lower forms of life. Hence the acts themselves which are proper to conjugal love and which are exercised in accord with genuine human dignity must be honored with great reverence (CCMW, N. 51).

25.
Therefore when there is question of harmonizing conjugal love with the responsible transmission of life, the moral aspect of any procedure does not depend solely on sincere intentions or on an evaluation of motives. It must be determined by objective standards. These, based upon the nature of the human person and his acts, preserve the full sense of mutual self-giving and human procreation in the context of true love. Such a goal cannot be achieved unless the virtue of conjugal chastity is sincerely practiced. Relying on these principles,

sons of the Church may not undertake methods of regulating procreation which are found blameworthy by the teaching authority of the Church in its unfolding of the divine law (CCMW, N. 51).

26.
Everyone should be persuaded that human life and the task of transmitting it are not realities bound up with this world alone. Hence they cannot be measured or perceived only in terms of it, but always have a bearing on the eternal destiny of men (CCMW, N. 51).

Marriage: A Path to Holiness

27.
Finally, let the spouses themselves, made to the image of the living God and enjoying the authentic dignity of persons, be joined to one another in equal affection, harmony of mind, and the work of mutual sanctification. Thus they will follow Christ who is the principle of life. Thus, too, by the joys and sacrifices of their vocation and through their faithful love, married people will become witnesses of the mystery of that love which the Lord revealed to the world by His dying and His rising up to life again (CCMW, N. 52).

28.
Married couples and Christian parents should follow their own proper path to holiness by faithful love, sustaining one another in grace throughout the entire length of their lives. They should imbue their offspring, lovingly welcomed from God, with Christian truths and evangelical virtues. For thus they can offer to all men an example of unwearying and generous love, build up the brotherhood of charity, and stand as witnesses to and cooperators

in the fruitfulness of holy Mother Church. By such lives, they signify and share in that very love with which Christ loved His bride and because of which He delivered himself up on her behalf. A like example, but one given in a different way, is that offered by widows and single people, who are able to make great contributions toward holiness and apostolic endeavor in the Church (DCC, N. 41).

29.
Christian husbands and wives are cooperators in grace and witnesses of faith on behalf of each other, their children, and all others in their household. They are the first to communicate the faith to their children and to educate them; by word and example they train their offspring for the Christian and apostolic life. They prudently help them in the choice of their vocation and carefully promote any religious calling which they may discern in them (DAL, N. 11).

30.
It has always been the duty of Christian couples, but today it is the supreme task of their apostolate, to manifest and prove by their own way of life the unbreakable and sacred character of the marriage bond, to affirm vigorously the right and duty of parents and guardians to educate children in a Christian manner, and to defend the dignity and lawful independence of the family. They and the rest of the faithful, therefore, should cooperate with men of good will to ensure the preservation of these rights in civil legislation, and to make sure that attention is paid to the needs of the family in government policies regarding housing, the education of children, working conditions, social security, and taxes; and that in decisions

affecting migrants their right to live together as a family is safeguarded (DAL, N. 11).

31.
Finally, Christian spouses, in virtue of the sacrament of Matrimony, signify and partake of the mystery of that unity and fruitful love which exists between Christ and His Church (cf. Eph. 5:32). The spouses thereby help each other to attain to holiness in their married life and by the rearing and education of their children. And so, in their state and order of life, they have their own special gift among the People of God (cf. 1 Cor. 7:7) (DCC, N. 11).

POINTS TO PONDER

Why is the apostolate of married people uniquely important for the Church and society? (1 through 5)

What is implied in the marriage covenant of conjugal love? (6 through 17)

What is the true goal of conjugal love? (18 through 21)

What stance should married people take regarding the transmission of life? (22 through 26)

How do married people bear witness to Christ's love for His Church? (27 through 31)

NOVEMBER: FAMILY LIFE

SYNOPSIS

The family is the domestic Church. In it multiple activities of the apostolate can be carried on. It is the primary cell of society, whose well-being is extensively dependent upon the health of its family communities.

Parents have as their proper mission the task of transmitting life. While others may advise them in this matter, they themselves must decide before God when it is their duty to procreate.

The family is a school of deep humanity with both parents contributing to the formation of their children. The loving concern lavished on them by their father and mother must find an echo in the reverence and respect children give to their parents. In this way the Christian family will manifest to men the Savior's presence in the world.

Because family life is the foundation of society, public authority has a serious duty to promote the prosperity of the families under its charge. All Christians, especially those skilled in the required professions, together with priests and others dedicated to families, must support the solid establishment and healthy growth of family life.

Parents are the first and foremost educators of their children. Their role is so decisive that nothing can adequately substitute for it. They should have perfect freedom in the choice of school and religious education they give their children, and the government must protect their freedom in this matter. Especially must parents teach their children to love God and their neighbors, and prepare them to take their place in civil society and in the People of God.

DEVELOPMENT

God has established the family as the primary cell of society (1 and 2).

Laymen must hold in high esteem their task of transmitting life (3 through 7).

Family life is a school of Christian formation (8 through 12).

All men should work for the welfare of marriage and the family (13 through 18).

Parents are primarily responsible for the education of their children (19 through 23).

Public authority must allow parents to send their children to the school of their choice (24 through 27).

Parents must prepare their children to be good citizens of the Church and state (28 through 30).

NOVEMBER
FAMILY LIFE

Family Is Primary Cell of Society

1.

For from the wedlock of Christians there comes the family, in which new citizens of human society are born. By the grace of the Holy Spirit received in Baptism these are made children of God, thus perpetuating the People of God through the centuries. The family is, so to speak, the domestic Church. In it parents should, by their word and example, be the first preachers of the faith to their children. They should encourage them in the vocation which is proper to each of them, fostering with special care any religious vocation (DCC, N. 11).

2.

The family has received from God its mission to be the first and vital cell of society. It will fulfill this mission if it shows itself to be the domestic sanctuary of the Church through the mutual affection of its members and the common prayer they offer to God, if the whole family is caught up in the liturgical worship of the Church, and if it provides active hospitality and promotes justice and other good works for the service of all the brethren in need. Among the multiple activities of the family apostolate may be enumerated the following: the adoption of abandoned infants, hospitality to strangers, assistance in the operation of schools, helpful advice and material assistance to adolescents, help to engaged couples in preparing themselves better for marriage, catechetical work, support of married couples and families involved in material and moral crises, help for the aged not only by providing them with the necessities of life but also by obtaining for them a fair share of the benefits of economic progress (DAL, N. 11).

Respect for Task of Transmitting Life

3.

The well-being of the individual person and of human and Christian society is intimately linked with the healthy condition of that community produced by marriage and family. Hence Christians and all men who hold this community in high esteem sincerely rejoice in the various ways by which men today find help in fostering this community of love and perfecting its life, and by which spouses and parents are assisted in their lofty calling. Those who rejoice in such aids look for additional benefits from them and labor to bring them about (CCMW, N. 47).

4.

Parents should regard as their proper mission the task of transmitting human life and educating those to whom it has been transmitted. They should realize that they are thereby cooperators with the love of God the creator, and are, so to speak, the interpreters of that love. Thus they will fulfill their task with human and Christian responsibility. With docile reverence toward God, they will come to the right decision by common counsel and effort (CCMW, N. 50).

5.

They will thoughtfully take into account both their own welfare and that of their children, those already born and those which may be foreseen.

For this accounting they will reckon with both the material and the spiritual conditions of the times as well as of their state in life. Finally, they will consult the interests of the family group, of temporal society, and of the Church herself (CCMW, N. 50).

6.
The parents themselves should ultimately make this judgment in the sight of God. But in their manner of acting, spouses should be aware that they cannot proceed arbitrarily. They must be governed always according to a conscience dutifully conformed to the divine law itself, and should be submissive toward the Church's teaching office, which authentically interprets that law in the light of the Gospel. That divine law reveals and protects the integral meaning of conjugal love, and impels it toward a truly human fulfillment (CCMW, N. 50).

7.
Thus, trusting in divine providence and refining the spirit of sacrifice, married Christians glorify the creator and strive toward fulfillment in Christ when, with a generous human and Christian sense of responsibility, they acquit themselves of the duty to procreate. Among the couples who fulfill their God-given task in this way, those merit special mention who with wise and common deliberation, and with a gallant heart, undertake to bring up suitably even a relatively large family (CCMW, N. 50).

Christian Formation through Family Life
8.
As a result, with parents leading the way by example and family prayer, children and indeed every-

one gathered around the family hearth will find a readier path to human maturity, salvation, and holiness. Graced with the dignity and office of fatherhood and motherhood, parents will energetically acquit themselves of a duty which devolves primarily on them, namely, education, and especially religious education (CCMW, N. 48).

9.
As living members of the family, children contribute in their own way to making their parents holy. For they will respond to the kindness of their parents with sentiments of gratitude, with love and trust. They will stand by them as children should when hardships overtake their parents and old age brings its loneliness. Widowhood, accepted bravely as a continuation of the marriage vocation, will be esteemed by all. Families will share their spiritual riches generously with other families too (CCMW, N. 48).

10.
Thus the Christian family, which springs from marriage as a reflection of the loving covenant uniting Christ with the Church, and as a participation in that covenant, will manifest to all men the Savior's living presence in the world, and the genuine nature of the Church. This the family will do by the mutual love of the spouses, by their generous fruitfulness, their solidarity and faithfulness, and by the loving ways in which all members of the family work together (CCMW, N. 48).

11.
The family is a kind of school of deeper humanity. But if it is to achieve the full flowering of its life and mission, it needs the kindly communion of

minds and the joint deliberation of spouses, as well as the painstaking cooperation of parents in the education of their children. The active presence of the father is highly beneficial to their formation. The children, especially the younger among them, need the care of their mother at home. This domestic role of hers must be safely preserved, though the legitimate social progress of women should not be underrated on that account (CCMW, N. 52).

12.
Children should be so educated that as adults they can, with a mature sense of responsibility, follow their vocation, including a religious one, and choose their state in life. If they marry, they can thereby establish their family in favorable moral, social, and economic conditions. Parents and guardians should by prudent advice provide guidance to their young with respect to founding a family, and the young ought to listen gladly. At the same time no pressure, direct or indirect, should be put on the young to make them enter marriage or choose a specific partner (CCMW, N. 52).

Work for Welfare of Marriage and Family
13.
Thus the family is the foundation of society. In it the various generations come together and help one another to grow wiser and to harmonize personal rights with the other requirements of social life. All those, therefore, who exercise influence over communities and social groups should work efficiently for the welfare of marriage and the family (CCMW, N. 52).

14.
Public authority should regard it as a sacred duty to recognize, protect, and promote their authentic nature, to shield public morality, and to favor the prosperity of domestic life. The right of parents to beget and educate their children in the bosom of the family must be safeguarded. Children, too, who unhappily lack the blessing of a family should be protected by prudent legislation and various undertakings, and provided with the help they need (CCMW, N. 52).

15.
Redeeming the present time, and distinguishing eternal realities from their changing expressions, Christians should actively promote the values of marriage and the family, both by their example in their own lives and by cooperation with other men of good will. Thus when difficulties arise, Christians will provide, on behalf of family life, those necessities and helps which are suitably modern. To this end, the Christian instincts of the faithful, the upright moral consciences of men, and the wisdom and experience of persons versed in the sacred sciences will have much to contribute (CCMW, N. 52).

16.
Those, too, who are skilled in other sciences, notably the medical, biological, social, and psychological, can considerably advance the welfare of marriage and the family, along with peace of conscience, if by pooling their efforts they labor to explain more thoroughly the various conditions favoring a proper regulation of births (CCMW, N. 52).

17.

It devolves on priests duly trained about family matters to nurture the vocation of spouses by a variety of pastoral means, by preaching God's Word, by liturgical worship, and by other spiritual aids to conjugal and family life; to sustain them sympathetically and patiently in difficulties, and to make them courageous through love. Thus families which are truly noble will be formed (CCMW, N. 52).

18.

Various organizations, especially family associations, should try by their programs of instruction and action to strengthen young people and spouses themselves, particularly those recently wed, and to train them for family, social, and apostolic life (CCMW, N. 52).

Parents Responsible for Education

19.

Since parents have conferred life on their children, they have a most solemn obligation to educate their offspring. Hence parents must be acknowledged as the first and foremost educators of their children. Their role as educators is so decisive that scarcely anything can compensate for their failure in it. For it devolves on parents to create a family atmosphere so animated with love and reverence for God and men that a well-rounded personal and social development will be fostered among the children. Hence, the family is the first school of those social virtues which every society needs (DCE, N. 3).

20.
The family is, as it were, the primary mother and nurse of this attitude. There in an atmosphere of love, children can more easily learn the true structure of reality. There, too, tested forms of human culture impress themselves upon the mind of the developing adolescent in a kind of automatic way (CCMW, N. 61).

21.
Opportunities for the same kind of education can also be found in modern society, thanks especially to the increased circulation of books and to the new means of cultural and social communication. All such opportunities can foster a universal culture (CCMW, N. 61).

22.
Since the family is a society in its own original right, it has the right freely to live its own domestic religious life under the guidance of parents. Parents, moreover, have the right to determine, in accordance with their own religious beliefs, the kind of religious education that their children are to receive (DRF, N. 5).

23.
In the family, parents have the task of training their children from childhood to recognize God's love for all men. Especially by example they should teach them little by little to show concern for the material and spiritual needs of their neighbor. The whole of family life, then, would become a sort of apprenticeship for the apostolate (DAL, N. 30).

Parents Free to Choose School of Choice

24.

Parents, who have the first and the inalienable duty and right to educate their children, should enjoy true freedom in their choice of schools. Consequently, public authority, which has the obligation to oversee and defend the liberties of citizens, ought to see to it, out of a concern for distributive justice, that public subsidies are allocated in such a way that, when selecting schools for their children, parents are genuinely free to follow their consciences (DCE, N. 6).

25.

Let the faithful labor and collaborate with all others in the proper regulation of the affairs of economic and social life. With special care, let them devote themselves to the education of children and young people by means of different kinds of schools. These schools should be considered not only as an outstanding means for forming and developing Christian youth, but also as a service of supreme value to men, especially in the developing nations, a service elevating the level of human dignity, and preparing the way for living conditions which are more humane (DCMA, N. 12).

26.

As for Catholic parents, the Council calls to mind their duty to entrust their children to Catholic schools, when and where this is possible, to support such schools to the extent of their ability, and to work along with them for the welfare of their children (DCE, N. 8).

27.

Government, in consequence, must acknowledge the right of parents to make a genuinely free choice of schools and of other means of education. The use of this freedom of choice is not to be made a reason for imposing unjust burdens on parents, whether directly or indirectly. Besides, the rights of parents are violated if their children are forced to attend lessons or instructions which are not in agreement with their religious beliefs. The same is true if a single system of education, from which all religious formation is excluded, is imposed upon all (DRF, N. 5).

Parents' Responsibility to Form
Good Citizens of Church and State

28.

Parents and teachers and all who are in any way engaged in the education of boys and young men should so prepare them that, recognizing the Lord's concern for His flock, and considering the needs of the Church, they will be ready to respond generously to our Lord if He should call, and will say with the prophet: "Lo, here am I, send me" (Is. 6:8) (DMLP, N. 11).

29.

Parents should be mindful of their duty to guard against shows, publications, and the like which would jeopardize faith or good morals. Let them see that such things never cross the thresholds of their homes and that their children do not encounter them elsewhere (DISC, N. 10).

30.

It is particularly in the Christian family, enriched by the grace and the office of the sacrament of

Matrimony, that from their earliest years children should be taught, according to the faith received at Baptism, to have a knowledge of God, to worship Him, and to love their neighbor. Here, too, they gain their first experience of wholesome human companionship and of the Church. Finally, it is through the family that they gradually are introduced into civic partnership with their fellow-men, and into the People of God. Let parents, then, clearly recognize how vital a truly Christian family is for the life and development of God's own people (DCE, N. 3).

POINTS TO PONDER

In what sense is the family the first vital cell in society? (1 through 3)

By what principles should parents decide to procreate children? (4 through 7)

How do parents and children assist each other in attaining holiness? (8 through 13)

What means are available to assure the prosperity of family life? (14 through 18)

What rights do parents have regarding the education of their children? (19 through 21)

What safeguards should parents enjoy concerning the religious formation of their children? (22 through 27)

Why is Christian family life vital for the development of God's People? (28 through 30)

DECEMBER: VARIOUS VOCATIONS

SYNOPSIS

One and the same holiness vivifies the apostolate through the Holy Spirit who makes laymen conscious of their responsibility to serve Christ in the Church. But if they are to do so effectively they need the necessary spiritual and technical formation. Properly prepared, they can make significant contributions to society.

Workers of all classes, including women, should be able to find suitable employment without discrimination; at times this will demand some control over economic affairs. Farmers, laborers, and workers of all types need opportunities to develop their talents and use their leisure time for healthful relaxation. Today men can be freed from the misery of ignorance.

Laymen should be encouraged to enter the field of social communications, including the news media and fine arts. There they can exert great influence on men and ideas.

Teachers in all levels of education have a serious responsibility to see that the building of the earthly city has its foundation in God. Young persons, properly formed, can exert substantial influence on modern society, particularly by a direct apostolate to other young people. Adults in the organized apostolates can attract young members by their own zealous activities.

All who are oppressed or suffer in any way must be taught that they can be united with the suffering Christ for the salvation of the world. The Lord, as the destiny of human history, is drawing all men to himself, finally to reward each man according to his works.

DEVELOPMENT

One holiness sanctifies all the members of Christ (1 and 2).

All laymen are called to serve Christ in the Church (3 through 6).

Workers must be adequately cared for in all walks of life (7 through 14).

All men have the right to develop their full capabilities (15 and 16).

Opportunities for the apostolate abound in the communications fields (17 through 21).

Artists are called to imitate the creator in their work (22 and 23).

Teachers must develop a sense of God's presence in their students (24 through 26).

Young people can exercise substantial influence on society (27 through 29).

All men can work with Christ for the salvation of the world (30 and 31).

DECEMBER
VARIOUS VOCATIONS

One Holiness Sanctifies All

1.

In the various types and duties of life, one and the same holiness is cultivated by all who are moved by the Spirit of God, and who obey the voice of the Father, worshiping God the Father in spirit and truth. These souls follow the poor Christ, the humble and cross-bearing Christ, in order to be worthy of being partakers in His glory. Every person should walk unhesitatingly according to his own personal gifts and duties in the path of a living faith which arouses hopes and works through charity (DCC, N. 41).

2.

All of Christ's faithful, therefore, whatever be the conditions, duties, and circumstances of their lives, will grow in holiness day by day through these very situations, if they accept them all with faith from the hand of their heavenly Father, and if they cooperate with the divine will by showing every man through their earthly activities the love with which God has loved the world (DCC, N. 41).

Call to Serve Christ in the Church

3.

An indication of this manifold and pressing need is the unmistakable work of the Holy Spirit in making the laity even more conscious of their own responsibility today and inspiring them everywhere to serve Christ and the Church (DAL, N. 1).

4.

If they are to shoulder all these tasks, laymen need the necessary technical and spiritual preparation. Such preparation should be given in institutes established for this purpose. Thus their lives will give witness to Christ among the non-Christians, according to the words of the Apostle: "Do not be a stumbling block to Jews and Gentiles and to the Church of God, even as I myself in all things please all men, not seeking what is profitable to myself but to the many, that they may be saved" (1 Cor. 10:32, 33) (DCMA, N. 41).

5.

Women are now employed in almost every area of life. It is appropriate that they should be able to assume their full proper role in accordance with their own nature. Everyone should acknowledge and favor the proper and necessary participation of women in cultural life (CCMW, N. 60).

6.

If the demands of justice and equity are to be satisfied, vigorous efforts must be made, without violence to the rights of persons or to the natural characteristics of each country, to remove as quickly as possible the immense economic inequalities which now exist. In many cases, these are worsening and are connected with individual and group discrimination (CCMW, N. 66).

Care for Workers in All Walks of Life

7.

In those economic affairs which are today subject to change, as in the new forms of industrial society in which automation, for example, is advancing, care must be taken that sufficient and suitable work can be obtained, along with appropriate technical and professional formation. The livelihood and the human dignity of those especially who are in particularly difficult circumstances because of illness or old age should be safeguarded (CCMW, N. 66).

8.
Justice and equity likewise require that the mobility which is necessary in a developing economy be regulated in such a way as to keep the life of individuals and their families from becoming insecure and precarious. Hence, when workers come from another country or district and contribute by their labor to the economic advancement of a nation or region, all discrimination with respect to wages and working conditions must be carefully avoided (CCMW, N. 66).

9.
The local people, moreover, especially public authorities, should all treat them not as mere tools of production but as persons, and must help them to arrange for their families to live with them and to provide themselves with decent living quarters. The natives should also see that these workers are introduced into the social life of the country or region which receives them. Employment opportunities, however, should be created in their own areas as far as possible (CCMW, N. 66).

10.
In many areas, too, farmers experience special difficulties in raising products or in selling them. In such cases, country people must be helped to increase and to market what they produce, to make the necessary advances and changes, and to

obtain a fair return. Otherwise, as too often happens, they will remain in the condition of lower-class citizens. Let farmers, especially young ones, skillfully apply themselves to perfecting their professional competence. Without it, no agricultural progress can take place (CCMW, N. 66).

11.

Today, more than ever before, progress in the production of agricultural and industrial goods and in the rendering of services is rightly aimed at making provision for the growth of a people and at meeting the rising expectations of the human race. Therefore, technical progress must be fostered, along with a spirit of initiative, an eagerness to create and expand enterprises, the adaptation of methods of production, and the strenuous efforts of all who engage in production — in a word, all the elements making for such development (CCMW, N. 64).

12.

Finally, laborers, whose work is often toilsome, should by their human exertions try to perfect themselves, aid their fellow citizens, and raise all of society, and even creation itself, to a better mode of existence. By their daily charity, joyous hope, and sharing of one another's burdens, let them also truly imitate Christ, who roughened His hands with carpenter's tools, and who in union with His Father is always at work for the salvation of all men. By their daily work itself laborers can achieve greater apostolic sanctity (DCC, N. 41).

13.

The opportunity should also be afforded to workers to develop their own abilities and personalities through the work they perform. Though they should apply their time and energy to their employment with a due sense of responsibility, all workers should also enjoy sufficient rest and leisure to cultivate their family, cultural, social, and religious life. They should also have the opportunity to develop on their own the resources and potentialities to which, perhaps, their professional work gives but little scope (CCMW, N. 67).

14.

The widespread reduction in working hours, for instance, brings increasing advantages to numerous people. May these leisure hours be properly used for relaxation of spirit and the strengthening of mental and bodily health. Such benefits are available through spontaneous study and activity and through travel, which refines human qualities and enriches men with mutual understanding. These benefits are obtainable too from physical exercise and sports events, which can help to preserve emotional balance, even at the community level, and to establish fraternal relations between men of all conditions, nations, and races. Hence let Christians work together to animate the cultural expressions and group activities of our times with a human and a Christian spirit (CCMW, N. 61).

The Right to Develop Full Capabilities

15.

The possibility now exists of liberating most men from the misery of ignorance. Hence it is a duty most befitting our times that men, especially Christians, should work strenuously on behalf of certain decisions which must be made in the economic and political fields, both nationally and internationally. By these decisions universal recognition and implementation should be given to the right of all men to a human and civic culture favorable to personal dignity and free from any discrimination on the grounds of race, sex, nationality, religious, or social conditions (CCMW, N. 60).

16.
Energetic efforts must also be expended to make everyone conscious of his right to culture and of the duty he has to develop himself culturally and to assist others. For existing conditions of life and of work sometimes thwart the cultural strivings of men and destroy in them the desire for self-improvement. This is especially true of country people and laborers. They need to be provided with working conditions which will not block their human development but rather favor it (CCMW, N. 60).

Opportunities Abound in Communications
17.
First of all, laymen should be instructed in art, doctrine, and ethics. Such a goal requires an increased number of schools, faculties, and institutes in which movie, radio, and television writers, journalists, and other concerned persons can obtain rounded formation animated by a Christian spirit, especially with regard to the Church's social doctrine. Theatrical actors should be trained and helped so that by their artistry they may enrich human culture with their own special gifts. Finally, active preparation should be given to critics in the literary, movie, radio, and television, and other fields, so that each may know his own specialty superbly and be taught and inspired to make judgments in which moral issues are always presented in their proper light (DISC, N. 15).

18.

With common heart and mind, let all the sons of the Church strive immediately and most energetically to use the instruments of social communication effectively in the many fields of the apostolate, as the circumstances and the times require. These efforts should head off hurtful enterprises, especially in those places where moral and religious needs dictate a more active zeal (DISC, N. 13).

19.

The chief moral duties respecting the proper use of instruments of social communication fall on newsmen, writers, actors, designers, producers, exhibitors, distributors, operators, and sellers, critics, and whoever else may have a part of any kind in making and transmitting products of communication. For it is quite clear what heavy responsibilities are given to all such persons in the present state of affairs. By molding and activating the human race they can lead it upward or to ruin. On these persons, then, will lie the task of regulating the commercial, political, and artistic aspects of these media in ways which will never conflict with the common good. They will merit praise if they aim to secure this goal more certainly by joining professional groups which expect from their members reverence for moral laws in the affairs and regulations of their art. If necessary, these associations should require adherence to a code of ethical conduct (DISC, N. 11).

20.

Likewise, let effective backing be given to decent radio and television productions, particularly those which are proper family fare. Catholic features should be intelligently encouraged, that through them audiences may be led to participate in the Church's life, and truths of religion may be instilled. When the opportunity presents itself, efforts should be made to establish Catholic stations. It should be a matter of concern that their offerings excel in professional quality and forcefulness. Let efforts be expended to see that the noble and ancient art of the theater, now widely popularized through the instruments of social communication, serve the cultural and moral development of audiences (DISC, N. 14).

21.

The production and showing of films which serve honest relaxation as well as culture and art, especially those meant for young people, should be promoted and guaranteed by every effective means. Catholics can see to this especially by supporting and even joining those forces and enterprises which involve honorable producers and distributors; by commending praiseworthy films through critical acclaim and awards; by patronizing theaters managed by upright Catholics and others — theaters which would do well to form associations (DISC, N. 14).

Artists Called to Imitate Christ

22.

All artists, who, in view of their talents, desire to serve God's glory in holy Church should ever bear in mind that they are engaged in a kind of sacred imitation of God the Creator, and are concerned with works destined for use in Catholic worship and for the edification, devotion, and religious instruction of the faithful (CSL, N. 127).

23.

Composers, filled with the Christian spirit, should feel that their vocation is to cultivate sacred music and increase its store of treasures. Let them produce compositions which have the qualities proper to genuine sacred music, not confining themselves to works which can be sung only by large choirs, but providing also for the needs of small choirs and for the active participation of the entire assembly of the faithful (CSL, N. 121).

Teachers To Develop Sense of God's Presence

24.

Worthy of special praise are those laymen who work in universities or in scientific institutes and whose historical and scientific religious research promotes knowledge of peoples and of religion. Thus they help the heralds of the Gospel, and prepare for dialogue with non-Christians. They should cooperate in a brotherly spirit with other Christians, with non-Christians, and with members of international organizations, having always before their eyes the fact that "the building up of the earthly city should have its foundation in the Lord, and should be directed toward Him" (*Dogmatic Constitution on the Church*, N. 46) (DCMA, N. 41).

25.

Beautiful, therefore, and truly solemn is the vocation of all those who assist parents in fulfilling their task, and who represent human society as well, by undertaking the role of school teacher. This calling requires extraordinary qualities of mind and heart, extremely careful preparation, and a constant readiness to begin anew and to adapt (DCE, N. 5).

26.

Above all, let them perform their services as partners of the parents. Together with them, they should pay due regard in every educational activity to sexual differences and to the special role which divine Providence allots to each sex in family life and in society. Let them work strenuously to inspire personal initiative on their students' part. Even after students have graduated, their teachers should continue to assist them with advice and friendship and also by establishing special groups genuinely inspired by the spirit of the Church. This holy Synod asserts that the ministry of such teachers is a true apostolate, which our times makes extremely serviceable and necessary, and which simultaneously renders an authentic service to society (DCE, N. 8).

Influence of Young on Society

27.

Young persons exert substantial influence on modern society. There has been a complete change in the circumstances of their lives, their mental attitudes, and their relationships with their families. Frequently they move too quickly into new social and economic conditions. While their social and even their political importance is growing from day to day, they seem unable to cope adequately with the new burdens imposed upon them (DAL, N. 12).

28.

Their heightened influence in society demands of them a proportionately active apostolate. Happily, their natural qualities fit them for this activity. As they become more conscious of their own personality, they are impelled by a zest for life and abounding energies to assume their own responsibility, and they yearn to play their part in social and cultural life. If this zeal is imbued with the spirit of Christ and is inspired by obedience to and love for the shepherds of the Church, it can be expected to be very fruitful. They themselves ought to become the prime and direct apostles of youth, exercising the apostolate among themselves and through themselves and reckoning with the social environment in which they live (DAL, N. 12).

29.

Adults ought to engage in friendly discussion with young people so that both groups, overcoming the age barrier, can become better acquainted and can share the special benefits each generation has to offer the other. Adults should attract young persons to the apostolate first by good example, and, if the opportunity presents itself, by offering them balanced advice and effective assistance. For their part, young people would be wise to cultivate toward adults respect and trust. Although the young are naturally attracted to new things, they should exercise an intelligent regard for worthwhile traditions. Children also have their own apostolic work to do. In their own way, they can be true living witnesses to Christ among their companions (DAL, N. 12).

All to Work for Salvation of the World

30.

Those who are oppressed by poverty, infirmity, sickness, or various other hardships, as well as those who suffer persecution for justice' sake — may they all know that in a special way they are united with the suffering Christ for the salvation of the world. The Lord called them blessed in His Gospel. They are those whom "the God of all grace, who has called us unto his eternal glory in Christ Jesus, will himself, after we have suffered a little while, perfect, strengthen, and establish" (1 Peter 5:10) (DCC, N. 41).

31.
For God's Word, by whom all things were made, was himself made flesh so that as perfect Man He might save all men and sum up all things in himself. The Lord is the goal of human history, the focal point of the longings of history and of civilization, the center of the human race, the joy of every heart, and the answer to all its yearnings. He it is whom the Father raised from the dead, lifted up on high, and stationed at His right hand, making Him judge of the living and the dead. Enlivened and united in His Spirit, we journey toward the consummation of human history, one which fully accords with the counsel of God's love: "To reestablish all things in Christ, both those in the heavens and those on the earth" (Eph. 1:10).

The Lord himself speaks: "Behold, I come quickly! And my reward is with me, to render to each one according to his works. I am the Alpha and the Omega, the first and the last, the beginning and the end" (Rev. 22:12, 13) (CCMW, N. 45).

POINTS TO PONDER

How can laymen grow daily in holiness? (1 through 5)

Why are economic conditions crucial for human development? (6 through 12)

How should leisure be used in today's world? (13 through 16)

How can laymen influence the instruments of communication? (17 through 21)

What role do artists play in the contemporary Church? (22 and 23)

How can teachers help to create a Christian society? (24 through 26)

In what way can young people serve as apostles? (27 through 29)

Why are all men able to assist Christ in saving the world? (30 and 31)